YOU HAVE NO RIGHTS

You Have No Rights

STORIES OF AMERICA IN AN AGE OF REPRESSION

Matthew Rothschild

THE NEW PRESS

NEW YORK
LONDON

Published in the United States by The New Press, New York, 2007
Distributed by W. W. Norton & Company, Inc., New York

LIBRARY OF CONGRESS CATALOGING-IN-PUBLICATION DATA
Rothschild, Matthew.
You have no rights : stories of America in an age of repression /
Matthew Rothschild.
p. cm.
ISBN 978-1-59558-16-8 (pbk.)
1. Political rights—United States.   2. Civil rights—United States.
3. Rule of law—United States.   4. Political persecution—United States.
5. Intelligence service—United States—Evaluation.   6. Terrorism—
United States—Prevention.   7. National security—Law and legislation—
United States.   8. United States—Politics and government—2001–   I. Title.
KF4749.R68 2007
342.7308'54–dc22
2006102480

The New Press was established in 1990 as a not-for-profit alternative
to the large, commercial publishing houses currently dominating
the book publishing industry. The New Press operates in the
public interest rather than for private gain, and is committed to publishing,
in innovative ways, works of educational, cultural, and community
value that are often deemed insufficiently profitable.

www.thenewpress.com

Composition by dix!
This book was set in Bell MT

Printed in Canada

2   4   6   8   10   9   7   5   3   1

To Jean,
and to Sam, Katherine, and Will,
and to my parents, Edward and Susan Rothschild,
believers in democracy

There is no doubt that if we lived in a police state, it would be easier to catch terrorists. If we lived in a country where the police were allowed to search your home at any time for any reason; if we lived in a country where the government is entitled to open your mail, eavesdrop on your phone conversations, or intercept your e-mail communications; if we lived in a country where people could be held in jail indefinitely based on what they write or think, or based on mere suspicion that they are up to no good, the government would probably discover and arrest more terrorists or would-be terrorists, just as it would find more lawbreakers generally. But that wouldn't be a country in which we would want to live, and it wouldn't be a country for which we could, in good conscience, ask our young people to fight and die. In short, that country wouldn't be America.

—Senator Russ Feingold, October 11, 2001,
in a debate over the Patriot Act.
Senator Feingold was the only senator to vote against it.

If this Nation is to remain true to the ideals symbolized by its flag, it must not wield the tools of tyrants.

—Supreme Court Justice John Paul Stevens,
writing in *Rumsfeld v. Padilla*, June 2004

Contents

Acknowledgments

This book would not have happened if my wonderful wife, Jean, had not encouraged me to do it and afforded me the time to get it done.

Nor would it have happened if Bob McChesney had not introduced me to Andy Hsiao, executive editor at The New Press, who shepherded me along with wisdom and care. I'd also like to thank Melissa Richards, Michelle Risley, and Sarah Fan of The New Press and the copy editor, Rachel Burd, for helping out along the way. It's been a pleasure. Thanks, too, to the great civil libertarian Nat Hentoff, who early on suggested that I put my writings between hard covers.

I owe a huge debt of gratitude to *The Progressive* magazine, where I have worked for the past twenty-four years. One of the most venerable voices for peace and justice in the country, it has given me enormous journalistic freedom and stimulation, along with a platform and a megaphone. I'd like to pay my respects to my predecessor, Erwin Knoll, who defended the First Amendment with tenacious delight, including when he was arrested for distributing copies of the Bill of Rights in a shopping mall. After 9/11 the staff encouraged me to put down my editing pen for a bit and report on the infringements of civil liberties that were—and still are—taking place. I'm grateful for the nudge. And thanks to all the e-mailers out there who have sent me tip after tip. Some of the reporting for this book first appeared in articles for *The Progressive*. Much of it ran originally on our Web site, www .progressive.org, in serial form, under "McCarthyism Watch." And *The Progressive* allowed me the time to do additional work for this book in the first half of 2006. Special thanks to the magazine's culture editor, Elizabeth DiNovella, for her editing suggestions, and to proofreader extraordinaire Diana Cook.

I'm also indebted to the civil liberties groups and lawyers that work so hard on these issues. The American Civil Liberties Union (ACLU) has done yeoman's duty since 9/11, and it has represented many of the people whose cases I chronicle. The Center for Constitutional Rights (CCR) has carried the ball on several urgent cases, especially those having to do with Bush's exercise of imperial power overseas and his trampling on the rights of detainees in his endless "war on terror." The valiant efforts by attorneys Barbara Olshansky, Rachel Meeropol, Michael Ratner, and David Cole cannot be overpraised. I'd like to especially thank David Cole for lending me guidance, and for his indispensable book *Enemy Aliens*. The National Lawyers Guild has also been helpful, and I've enjoyed participating on panels and at protests with their members. I've also benefited from the work of the Lawyers' Committee for Civil Rights Under Law, which helped me out on a story or two. The Council on American-Islamic Relations (CAIR) acted as a vital go-between for me, and its news releases and annual reports yielded crucial information. The American-Arab Anti-Discrimination Committee (ADC) and the Arab American Institute came in handy in my research. And the Sikh American Legal Defense and Education Fund proved useful, as well.

Last but not least, to the individuals who shared their stories with me, and who stood up and fought for their rights, you have my utmost gratitude and admiration. This is your book as much as mine.

—Madison, Wisconsin
January 31, 2007

YOU HAVE NO RIGHTS

Introduction

It was early October 2001. I was giving a talk to a group of about fifty peace activists up in Sauk City, about a half hour northwest of Madison, Wisconsin, where I live. At the end of my talk a woman raised her hand and asked me if I'd heard about Todd Persche.

"No, I'm sorry, who's Todd Persche?" I asked.

"He's a local cartoonist up here who just got fired," she told me.

For three years Persche had been drawing a weekly cartoon for the *Baraboo News Republic* at $25 a throw. Then, after September 11, he drew a couple that got him canned. One said, "When the media keeps pounding on the war drum . . . it's hard to hear other points of view." The other was about Big Brother "turning our civil rights upside down."

At that moment I figured I'd better start paying attention.

As Persche told me over the phone a few days later, "In these times, they make you feel like you're not a patriot just because you're dissenting."

So I looked around and I discovered stories about prizewinning columnists who were fired shortly after 9/11 just for doing their job. Dan Guthrie had been Oregon columnist of the year at the *Daily Courier* of Grants Pass. On September 15, 2001, he wrote an article entitled "When the Going Gets Tough, the Tender Turn Tail." In it he talked about how Bush had "skedaddled" away in an act of "cowardice." A week later the publisher fired Guthrie. And the editor issued a front-page apology: "This Is No Time to Criticize the Nation's Leader: Apology for Printing Column."

I found a few other examples and wrote them up for the cover story of the January 2002 issue of *The Progressive*, entitled "The New McCarthyism." And I thought that was that. On to the next story or back to editing. But even as the January 2002 issue was still at the printer, I got a call from a guy named Daniel Muller, the co-coordinator of Voices in the Wilderness, a group dedicated to nonviolence. He and a colleague had gone to their usual post office in Chicago and ordered four thousand stamps for a fund-raising mailing. Since most of the group's supporters have profound disagreements with the way the U.S. government behaves overseas, Muller specifically asked for non-American-flag stamps. The teller called the police on them. "Two cops came in and asked for our IDs," Muller told me. "They asked if we had any outstanding warrants. They ran a check on us. They asked us why we had asked for stamps without the American flags on them." Muller wasn't arrested. But he didn't get his stamps that day, either.

As I kept hearing more stories along these lines, I decided to keep track of them on *The Progressive*'s Web site, www.progressive.org. Focusing on this beat allowed me to get to some stories ahead of the pack, like the existence of the "no fly" list and the infiltration of police into peace groups.

This book is not a comprehensive compendium. I don't include even half of the stories I've reported on, and I'm sure there are hundreds of relevant stories I've never even heard of yet. I don't focus on the celebrities, who have received a lot of attention already. And I'm not including many other stories, some fairly well known, like the case of peace activist Cindy Sheehan, who was kicked out of the Capitol at the 2006 State of the Union address for wearing an antiwar T-shirt, or like Jay Bennish, the Colorado teacher who got into trouble for making a comparison between Bush and Hitler. When such stories did break, they were most often described as unique events, as anomalies. They were anything but.

We need to have memory; we need to see patterns. Those who are in power feast on our ignorance; they don't want us to have a memory longer than a single news cycle. They want our minds to drift, our eyes to wander. Then they can get away with just about anything. And so they have.

In this book I've grouped eighty-two of these stories so we can see the patterns. Since 9/11, innocent individuals just minding their own business or simply exercising their First Amendment freedoms have been deprived of their rights. As I've done my reporting it's become quite clear that those who have had it the hardest in this country are Arab Americans and Muslim Americans and those from South Asia, who have often been mistaken for Muslims. For these populations life in the United States has been qualitatively harsher. It is not America to them.

I chose as the title for this book a quote from an employee at the Metropolitan Detention Center in New York, who told detainee Yasser Ebrahim: "Forget about human rights. . . . You have no rights." Guards had badly abused Ebrahim and other detainees there. For Arabs and Muslims without citizenship in America, this title applies best. And it serves as a warning for all Americans, for George W. Bush has put policies in place that jeopardize the "first freedoms" of every U.S. citizen. I delineate some of those policies in the first chapter, "The Edifice of Repression."

But mostly, this is a book of stories: real people facing real hard-

ship because of who they are or the views they express. I can still hear
the anger and the pain, the befuddlement and disgust, in many of their
voices. I hope you hear those feelings, too.

By the way, I ran into Todd Persche at a bookstore in nearby Baraboo four years later. I was in a debate there with a Republican state
legislative aide about everything from the Iraq War to civil liberties to
religion. As I was leaving Persche introduced himself. I asked him if he
had been drawing any cartoons lately. He said, "No, I'm going to wait
until my kids are out of high school—just in case."

1

The Edifice of Repression

To those who scare peace-loving people with phantoms of lost liberty, my message is this: Your tactics only aid terrorists. . . . They give ammunition to America's enemies, and pause to America's friends.

—former attorney general John Ashcroft

You're either with us or against us.

—George W. Bush

Today's America is a much less free place than the America of 2000. Following the attacks of September 11, 2001, the Bush administration has, by word and by deed, erected an edifice of repression here in the United States.

We've been living in it ever since. And it's not a comfortable place.

The government is monitoring your phone calls and can read your e-mails and open your snail mail.

The government can access records of your large financial transactions, such as buying a house.

Law enforcement officers can bust into your home when you're not there, riffle through your belongings, plant a recording device on your computer, and leave without notifying you for at least thirty days—and maybe a lot more.

You no longer have the right to protest where the president or vice president can see you, or at major public events when they aren't even present.

Law enforcement officers can now monitor you in public if you are merely exercising your political rights.

They can infiltrate your political organizations.

And they can keep track of you at your place of worship.

The government can find out from bookstores and libraries the material you've been reading, and the bookstore owner and the librarian can't talk about it, except to their lawyers, for a whole year—or more.

The government can hold you in preventive detention for months on end as a "material witness."

If you're not a citizen the government can deport you on a technicality or for mere political association.

If you're not a citizen the government can label you an "enemy combatant" and send you to secret prisons around the world, where you may never see the light of day again—much less a lawyer or a judge.

And even if you are a citizen, the government can label you an enemy combatant and hold you in solitary confinement here in the United States.

Under George W. Bush's interpretation of the president's powers during the so-called war on terror he can do just about whatever he wants. He cites the Authorization for Use of Military Force bill, which Congress passed on September 18, 2001, as the justification for this enormous leeway.

"Congress gave me the authority to use necessary force to protect the American people, but it didn't prescribe the tactics," Bush said in a speech at Kansas State University on January 23, 2006. Those tactics, he presumes, are totally up to him. Under this rationale Bush could send F-16s to attack a residential area in, say, Indianapolis if he thought Al Qaeda suspects were there.

Lest you think I'm exaggerating, check out the February 13, 2006, issue of *Newsweek*:

> A Justice Department official suggested that in certain circumstances, the President might have the power to order the killing of terrorist suspects inside the United States. . . . Steven Bradbury, acting head of the department's Office of Legal Counsel, went to a closed-door Senate Intelligence committee meeting last week to defend President George W. Bush's surveillance program. During the briefing, said Administration and Capitol Hill officials (who declined to be identified because the session was private), California Democratic Sen. Dianne Feinstein asked Bradbury questions about the extent of Presidential powers to fight Al Qaeda; could Bush, for instance, order the killing of a Qaeda suspect known to be on U.S. soil? Bradbury replied that he believed Bush could indeed do this, at least in certain circumstances.

Yes, the U.S. government has a primary obligation to protect us all from another attack. But there needs to be a legal limit; there needs to be a respect for our Constitution and our liberties. Otherwise, as Senator Russ Feingold pointed out, "this country won't be America."

What the Bush administration did after 9/11 was not to engage in precise police work to find any would-be terrorists in our midst. Instead, it issued edicts and enacted laws that curtailed all of our freedoms. And it cast a gigantic dragnet over Arabs and Muslims in this country, treating many of them with a de facto presumption of guilt.

The individual stories I tell in this book give an impressionistic account of what it's been like to live in the Bush age. To put those experiences in context we need to examine how the Bush administration constructed the edifice of repression.

It got the job done, in part, by blasting those who dared to dissent. When the president's former press secretary Ari Fleischer told people they should "watch what they say" after comedian Bill Maher on ABC's *Politically Incorrect* dared to question the label of "cowards" that Bush had slapped on the suicide bombers, it sent a message. As did the canceling of Maher's show. As did Bush's repeated assertion that "you're either with us or against us."

The message was clear: If you dissent you're un-American, you're a traitor.

And that message went down the ranks.

"You can make an easy kind of link that, if you have a protest group protesting a war where the cause that's being fought against is international terrorism, you might have terrorism at that protest," Mike Van Winkle, spokesman for the California Anti-Terrorism Information Center, told the *Oakland Tribune* in 2003. "You can almost argue that a protest against that is a terrorist act."

Celebrity dissenters, such as Susan Sarandon, Tim Robbins, Sean Penn, Linda Ronstadt, and the Dixie Chicks, all felt the sting of reprobation. The attacks on them reinforced the idea in the air that if you speak out, you'll pay a price. Gradually, as Bush's popularity has faded, his power to regulate the cultural thermostat has diminished.

But the Bush administration's efforts have gone way beyond chilly climate control. Breathtaking in its audaciousness, the administration has implemented, often by fiat, an amazing array of repressive policies that still stand. These policies deprive us of some of our most precious freedoms and threaten the very character of our democratic system.

This repression has not been indiscriminate. For the most part white, non-Muslim U.S. citizens have not felt the full brunt of it. But for many Muslim and Arab and South Asian immigrants in America, citizen or not, America became inhospitable overnight. Their quality of life, their sense of security, has never been the same.

1. The Ashcroft Raids

Just as the rounding up of ten thousand immigrants and radicals from 1918 to 1921 became known as the Palmer Raids, after Attorney General A. Mitchell Palmer, so too should the roundups after September 11 be called the Ashcroft Raids.

John Ashcroft, who served as attorney general from 2001 to 2005, sent law enforcement officers around the country to seize Muslims and Arabs in the United States and to hold them on whatever conceivable pretext. As David Cole notes in *Enemy Aliens*, this was a policy of "mass preventive detention." In the first two months after 9/11 the Ashcroft Raids had rounded up more than 1,182 people. (The Justice Department stopped reporting numbers after that.) Some were citizens; the majority were not.

Ashcroft sent law enforcement agents all over the country to nab immigrants on the slightest offenses. As he told the U.S. Conference of Mayors on October 25, 2001, "Let the terrorists among us be warned: If you overstay your visa—even by one day—we will arrest you. If you violate a local law, you will be put in jail and kept in custody as long as possible. We will use every available statute. We will seek every prosecutorial advantage."

Some Arabs and Muslims in the United States were apprehended solely on "anonymous tips called in by members of the public suspicious of Arab and Muslim neighbors who kept odd schedules," according to a June 2003 report of the Justice Department's Office of the

Inspector General titled "A Review of the Treatment of Aliens Held on Immigration Charges in Connection with the Investigation of the September 11 Attacks." One such detainee worked at a grocery store run by Middle Eastern men that was open twenty-four hours a day, and someone called that in as a threat, the report says. Three other Middle Eastern men were stopped in Manhattan on a traffic violation. In their car were design plans for a public school. Even though "their employers confirmed that the men were working on construction at the school and that it was appropriate for them to have the plans," they were detained.

"The Department was detaining aliens on immigration violations that generally had not been enforced in the past," the report noted. And it was detaining them for long periods of time, without the usual due process.

Before 9/11, the Immigration and Naturalization Service (INS) had a practice of charging detainees within forty-eight hours of their arrests. After the attacks, the INS changed that to seventy-two hours and added a huge loophole: "In the event of an emergency or other extraordinary circumstances, the charging decision could be made within an additional reasonable period of time," the inspector general's report said. That period was not specified, so there was no outer limit. More than 100 detainees were not charged within the first 10 days of detention, and 5 detainees waited "approximately 168 days after their arrest" to be charged. These delays "affected the detainees' ability to obtain effective legal counsel."

The detainees were held without bond. Many were labeled in an "indiscriminate and haphazard manner" by the FBI, making it difficult "to distinguish between aliens who it actually suspected of having a connection to terrorism as opposed to aliens who, while possibly guilty of violating federal immigration law, had no connection to terrorism." Many were held in the most restrictive wings of detention facilities.

And for the first "several days to several weeks" they were held incommunicado, not allowed to make any calls to lawyers or loved ones.

On average, the FBI held these detainees for 80 days before clearing them. One was actually held for 244 days: "The untimely clearance process had enormous ramifications for September 11 detainees."

One of those ramifications was brutalization.

At the Metropolitan Detention Center in Manhattan "there is evidence supporting the detainees' claims of abuse," the inspector general's report concluded. Detainees said officers "slammed them into walls, dragged them by their arms, stepped on the chain between their ankle cuffs . . . and twisted their arms, hands, wrists, and fingers." One detainee said that "an officer bent his finger back until it touched his wrist. Another said that "officers repeatedly twisted his arm, which was in a cast."

The Ashcroft Raids included not only the initial dragnet after September 11 but two other dragnets. One was the Absconder Apprehension Initiative. This program expressly targeted Arabs and Muslims for deportation, even though they made up only a tiny fraction of "the more than 300,000 foreign nationals living here with outstanding deportation orders," Cole writes in *Enemy Aliens*. The other was the Special Registration program, which ordered immigrant men from predominantly Muslim or Arab countries to report to the immigration service. According to Cole, these three dragnets combined rounded up more than 5,000 people.

With nothing to show for it.

"This program has been a colossal failure at finding terrorists," Cole writes. "Of the more than 5,000 persons subjected to preventive detention as of May 2003, not one has been charged with any involvement in the crimes of September 11."

The Center for Constitutional Rights filed a class-action lawsuit on behalf of "male non-citizens from the Middle East, South Asia, and elsewhere who are Arab or Muslim or have been perceived by Defendants to be Arab or Muslim, who have been arrested and detained on minor immigration violations" after 9/11. The suit, *Turkmen v. Ashcroft*, charged that their First, Fourth, Fifth, and Sixth Amendment rights were violated. (I profile two of the plaintiffs in the case in Chapter II.)

On June 14, 2006, District Judge John Gleeson dismissed the plaintiffs' claims, except those relating to the conditions of their confinement. He ruled that it was OK for the government to hold the detainees essentially on a pretext—a minor immigration infraction—when, in fact, they were holding them for other purposes. He said that it was OK for the government to hold detainees for six months—and sometimes longer—after a judge has issued a determination to deport. In fact, he said, the government could hold them so long as their release was "reasonably foreseeable"—an exceptionally elastic term.

And he said that it was OK for the government to discriminate on the basis of race, religion, and/or national origin by holding Muslim and Arab detainees longer than others. The judge cited a Supreme Court case (*Reno v. American-Arab Anti-Discrimination Committee*) that said that the discrimination needs to be "so outrageous" as to overcome the deference owed to the executive branch in immigration matters.

Judge Gleeson said there was nothing outrageous about the alleged discrimination in this case.

As Cole, who worked on the case with the Center for Constitutional Rights, pointed out in a *Los Angeles Times* piece, "In essence, he authorized a repeat of the Japanese internment."

2. *Abuse of Material Witness Statute*

The Bush administration has used another technique for holding people—primarily but not exclusively noncitizens—in preventive detention. And that is by aggressively and speciously applying the 1984 material witness statute. This law allows the government to detain a witness in a criminal case if it's likely that this person would flee before testifying.

Nat Hentoff wrote in *The Progressive*, this statute was "largely intended vent members of organized crime from fleeing."

But the Bus. tration used it to detain about four dozen people whom it viewed as s to charge with any crime or immigration violation. Some were held for more than three months, according to the Justice Department.

"Jailing people who are simply under investigation is a hallmark of an authoritarian regime," District Judge Shira Scheindlin ruled on April 30, 2002, in a case involving Osama Awadallah, a Jordanian student who was here legally but whose phone number was found in one of the 9/11 hijackers' cars. "If the government has probable cause to believe a person has committed a crime, it may arrest that person," Judge Scheindlin said. But misusing the material witness statute poses "the threat of making detention the norm and liberty the exception."

3. *Enemy Combatants and "Extraordinary Renditions"*

Another mechanism for depriving people—citizen and noncitizen alike—of their rights is to label them "enemy combatants." And that's what the Bush administration has been doing. It's held more than six hundred prisoners at Guantánamo Bay, Cuba, as enemy combatants, and it has held others the same way in Iraq and Afghanistan and in secret CIA prisons around the world. Using the ridiculous euphemism of "extraordinary renditions," the United States has seized hundreds of individuals and shipped them off to countries notorious for torture. (I profile one such person, Maher Arar, in Chapter VIII.)

In the process the Bush administration has deprived these detainees of their due process rights and denied them protection under the Geneva Conventions. In the Supreme Court's 2006 decision in *Hamdan v. Rumsfeld*, Justice John Paul Stevens, writing for the majority, ruled that Common Article 3 of the Geneva Conventions applies. That article requires trials by a "regularly constituted court, affording all the judicial guarantees which are recognized as indispensable by civilized peoples." Common Article 3 also prohibits "violence to life and person, in particular murder of all kinds, mutilation, cruel treatment and torture," as well as "outrages upon personal dignity, in particular humiliating and degrading treatment." (Similarly, Article 75, Fundamental Guarantees, of the 1977 protocol to the Geneva Conventions states unambiguously: "Persons who are in the power of a Party to the conflict and who do not benefit from more favorable treatment under the Conventions or under this Protocol shall be treated humanely in all circumstances.")

Essentially, the Bush administration claims the authority to seize any individual anywhere in the world, label that person an enemy combatant, and send him off to some prison in this remote corner or that, there to languish forever.

The Bush administration has used the enemy combatant label not only against foreign nationals but against U.S. citizens, too.

The administration held both Yasser Hamdi and José Padilla for more than two years, often in solitary confinement, in military brigs, and denied them their due process rights. They were held incommunicado and not charged with any crimes.

In one of its sillier arguments the Bush administration even claimed that it was holding Hamdi, who was picked up on a battlefield in Afghanistan, for his own benefit. The president, the government said in its Supreme Court brief, has "the authority to engage in the time-honored and humanitarian practice of *detaining* enemy combatants captured in connection with the conflict, as opposed to subjecting such combatants to the more harmful consequences of war" (italics in original).

Padilla, however, wasn't captured on the battlefield like Hamdi. He was collared at O'Hare Airport in Chicago. "By imprisoning Padilla *without a hearing of any sort* and *without producing any evidence against him*, the executive branch has taken one of the most drastic steps in our nation's history," writes Barbara Olshansky in *America's Disappeared*. (The italics in that quotation are hers.)

As it has with much of its overreaching, the Bush administration argued in the Hamdi and Padilla cases that the president's commander-in-chief powers in Article II of the Constitution give him the authority to designate citizens as enemy combatants and deprive them of due process. "You have to recognize that in a situation where there is a war, where the government is on a war footing, that you have to trust the executive," argued Paul Clement in *Hamdi*. Clement was deputy solicitor general at the time, and subsequently became solicitor general. Astonishingly, under questioning from the justices, Clement claimed that the president had this power to declare U.S. citizens enemy combatants even when there is no war. "The president had that authority on September tenth," Clement told the justices.

The Supreme Court disagreed, even about executive powers during wartime. As it said in the *Hamdi* decision, "A state of war is not a blank check for the President."

And in June 2006, in *Rasul v. Bush*, a case brought by Guantánamo detainees, the Supreme Court also ordered the government to give those detainees some due process protections. Nevertheless, the administration has dragged its feet.

As for Hamdi, the United States released and deported him in October 2004. As for Padilla, the Supreme Court decided not to rule on his original case, since they said his lawyers filed it in the wrong district. Then, rather than let the Supreme Court rule on his designation as an enemy combatant and risk repudiation, the Bush administration finally charged him with three crimes—more than three years after detaining him.

Justice John Paul Stevens, in the original Padilla case, let his views be known on the gravity of the matter. "At stake in the case is nothing less than the essence of a free society," he wrote. "Unconstrained Executive detention for the purpose of investigating and preventing subversive activity is the hallmark of the Star Chamber."

4. *Watering Down the Levi Guidelines: A Boon for Domestic Spying*

The Church Committee hearings (named after Senator Frank Church of Idaho) in 1974 and 1975 revealed widespread FBI spying on political dissidents. One of the FBI's most notorious counterintelligence programs was called COINTELPRO, which infiltrated and disrupted the Black Panthers and the American Indian Movement, among other groups. In response to the revelations President Gerald Ford had his attorney general, Edward Levi, draw up guidelines to limit such activities in the future. The 1976 Levi guidelines prohibited the FBI from investigating the First Amendment activities of individuals and groups that weren't advocating violence. And, mindful of the role of

FBI agents provocateurs in the 1960s, the guidelines outlawed the disruption of groups and the discrediting of individuals engaged in lawful First Amendment activities. Domestic spying could occur only when there was "specific and articulable facts" that indicated criminal activity.

Under the Reagan administration and that of Bush Senior, these guidelines were loosened somewhat. Then came Ashcroft.

On May 30, 2002, he threw out the need to demonstrate any connection to criminal activity. Ashcroft's guidelines allow the FBI "to engage in searches and monitoring of chat rooms, bulletin boards, and websites without evidence of criminal wrongdoing," notes the Electronic Privacy Information Center. "Additionally, agents are permitted to visit public places and events to monitor individuals' activities with no predicate of criminal suspicion. These powers are not limited to terrorism investigations." What's more, Ashcroft's guidelines "allow FBI agents to use private-sector databases prospectively in order to predict terrorist acts. These databases may be used without any evidence of criminal activity or suspicious behavior. The FBI can now go on data mining 'fishing trips.' "

And it's not just the FBI. Since 9/11, agents from the campus police all the way up to the National Guard and the Pentagon have gotten into the domestic snooping game. Much of the gathering of domestic intelligence has been done by joint terrorism task forces that bring together state and local law enforcement with the FBI.

A story that MSNBC broke on December 14, 2005, told how the Pentagon had been busy spying on antiwar groups. The Pentagon's own database lists forty-three events in a six-month period alone, dating from November 11, 2004, to May 7, 2005. Pentagon political spying took place in the following states and the District of Columbia: Arizona, Arkansas, California, Colorado, Connecticut, Florida, Georgia, Illinois, Louisiana, Massachusetts, Nebraska, New Jersey, New York, North Carolina, Ohio, Pennsylvania, Rhode Island, Texas, Vermont, and Wisconsin.

On January 17, 2007, the ACLU revealed that the Pentagon had monitored at least 186 antimilitary protests.

5. Listening In on Lawyer-Prisoner Conversations

Here's one of the violations of our civil liberties that has received little attention: If you're in federal custody you no longer can assume that you have the right to confidential communications with your lawyer.

On October 31, 2001, Ashcroft issued a regulation that allows the Justice Department at its own discretion and authority to eavesdrop on the lawyer-client conversations of anyone in its custody, so long as the attorney general says there is "reasonable suspicion" that the person in custody may use such conversations "to further or facilitate acts of terrorism." Prior to this, the only way prosecutors could eavesdrop on such communications was to demonstrate "probable cause" before a judge that the prisoner was using his discussions with counsel to further a criminal purpose. Under the Ashcroft regulation probable cause is no longer the standard. And Ashcroft unilaterally discarded the obligation of going to a judge. Now the executive branch itself makes the decision as to whether to listen in or not.

How can you possibly defend yourself and plan your legal strategy with your lawyer if the prosecutors are listening in?

"This regulation is an unprecedented frontal assault on the attorney-client privilege, and on the right to counsel and the right of access to the courts guaranteed by the Constitution," Nadine

Strossen, president of the ACLU, testified to the Senate Judiciary Committee on December 4, 2001.

6. *USA Patriot Act*

The USA Patriot Act, which passed the Senate by a vote of 98 to 1 and the House by a vote of 356 to 66, and was signed into law on October 26, 2001, established much of the legal framework for repression. With only two days of debate, Congress passed this mammoth bill, containing 1,016 separate sections. And while specific measures of the Patriot Act have received a lot of play in the media over the last five years, the very scope of the act has been neglected.

Under its broad definition of a domestic terrorist, Martin Luther King Jr. himself would have qualified, for it says someone is a domestic terrorist who engages in activities that

(A) involve acts dangerous to human life that are a violation of the criminal laws of the United States or of any State [and]

(B) appear to be intended:
   (i) to intimidate or coerce a civilian population
   (ii) to influence the policy of a government by intimidation or coercion; or
   (iii) to affect the conduct of a government by mass destruction, assassination, or kidnapping; and

(C) occur primarily within the territorial jurisdiction of the United States.

An aggressive prosecutor could easily have asserted that King, when he engaged in civil disobedience in Birmingham, was engaged in an act "dangerous to human life," since someone could have gotten run over. King certainly was in violation of the criminal laws of the state of Alabama. And the prosecutor could have asserted, with some ease, that King was trying "to intimidate or coerce a civilian population," since King was using every ounce of his moral suasion to get rid of Jim Crow. (J. Edgar Hoover could have only dreamed of such a law, since he had placed King under surveillance and was always looking for ways to discredit him.) An aggressive prosecutor in the future could use this statute to go after Greenpeace or Cindy Sheehan or other practitioners of the venerable American art of nonviolent civil disobedience.

The USA Patriot Act tramples on Fourth Amendment rights. First, Section 213 makes a mockery of the warrant process. This section allows for "sneak-and-peek" home invasions. The FBI does need a warrant, but you, as a citizen, have no right to inspect the warrant, which is one of the primary purposes for it in the first place. You should be able to go over the warrant and see whether the police are actually at the right location, and if they are not, you can challenge that warrant. But if law enforcement shows up when it knows you're not home, you're out of luck. Under the original Patriot Act, law enforcement officers did not even need to inform you that they had barged in as long as they continued to claim that you were still under investigation.

Second, the Patriot Act allows law enforcement the infamous power, under Section 215, to seize the records of any business—including bookstores and libraries—that has information about anyone with "relevance" to a national security investigation. Notice how low that threshold is. The FBI does not have to assert probable cause that someone has committed a crime or is a terrorist, but only that this person is relevant to a national security investigation. On top of that, any business hit with this demand for records had a gag order imposed on it for life. If you were a bookstore owner whom the FBI visited you could not tell anyone about it—ever.

For noncitizens, the USA Patriot Act is a nightmare. "It makes foreign nationals deportable for wholly innocent associational activity, excludable for pure speech, and subject to incarceration on the Attorney General's say-so," David Cole notes.

Section 411 of the USA Patriot Act allows the government to bar from this country those "who endorse or espouse terrorist activity." It doesn't define those terms, so the State Department has defined them incredibly loosely. The State Department's *Foreign Affairs Manual* (volume 9) interprets this to mean that people can be excluded for "irresponsible expressions of opinion." And even the spouse and the child of this irresponsible person can be made inadmissible to the United States, according to the Patriot Act itself. This is ideological exclusion that harkens back to the McCarran-Walter Act of 1952, which allowed the government to deport immigrants and naturalized citizens it deemed subversive, and to deny entry to the United States of anyone it claimed was subversive. Those it denied included Nobel Prize–winner Gabriel García Márquez, poet Pablo Neruda, and Pierre Trudeau before the last became prime minister of Canada.

Perhaps most egregiously the Patriot Act also allows virtually indefinite detention of noncitizens. Under Section 412, if the attorney general certifies that there are "reasonable grounds to believe that the alien . . . is engaged in any other activity that endangers the national security of the United States," the noncitizen can be held indefinitely. The only requirement the attorney general must meet is to stipulate every six months that "the release of the alien will threaten the national security of the United States or the safety of the community or any person."

7. *Revisions to the Patriot Act*

In early 2006 Congress made only "a few insignificant, face-saving changes" to the original Patriot Act, Senator Feingold notes.

For instance, on the question of obtaining library records or book-store records, the new law appears to let libraries off the hook, but then it snags them again. It says that libraries, when functioning in their traditional roles, are not subject to Section 215 orders. But it adds that libraries that provide "electronic communication services"—e-mail and perhaps simply Internet access—are subject. "So it is very unclear whether this section as now written provides any real protection to libraries," the American Library Association says.

Also, Congress did not change the standard for investigating someone under Section 215. That standard is still "relevance" to a terrorist investigation, though the Senate fought hard to raise that standard so that the person being investigated has some demonstrable connection to a terrorist.

The revised bill does reduce the lifetime gag order on businesses under Section 215 to one year. But this, too, is much less than meets the eye. To keep the gag on all the government has to do is tell a judge at the Foreign Intelligence Surveillance Court that there is reason to believe that lifting the gag "may endanger the national security of the U.S., interfere with a criminal, counterterrorism, or counterintelligence investigation, interfere with diplomatic relations, or endanger the life or physical safety of any person."

On the question of "sneak and peek," the only change is that the government now has to inform you of your home invasion within thirty days, though the government can get an unlimited number of ninety-day extensions on that notification.

As to the punitive measures relating to noncitizens, Congress did nothing. "Most of the act's worst provisions were not even on the table," Cole wrote in *The Nation* on April 3, 2006.

Congress actually made the Patriot Act worse in one respect: It gave the Secret Service more authority to curtail protests. The Secret Service has been in the pernicious habit of creating so-called free speech zones far from where the president or vice president is speaking. Now the Secret Service can designate something as a "special event of national significance" and thereby make it off-limits for its duration. It can cordon off such an event (e.g., a political convention, a meeting of the World Trade Organization), which may last for days, even when the president or the vice president has already left. The penalty for violating this is one year in prison, and if someone gets hurt while you are trying to protest within the restricted area, you can now face ten years.

8. National Security Letters

The USA Patriot Act, along with the 2004 Intelligence Authorization Act, greatly expanded the use of "national security letters." These letters are an extraordinarily powerful tool in the hands of the FBI. Basically, they amount to subpoenas the FBI issues by itself, without having to go to a judge for approval. When they were first authorized in 1978 to go after spies and terrorists the FBI was required to have " 'specific and articulable' reasons to believe the records it gathered in secret belonged to a terrorist or spy," Barton Gellman reported for the *Washington Post* on November 6, 2005. But now they can slap these executive branch subpoenas not only on terrorist suspects, but on anyone who is "relevant" to a national security investigation, even those "who are not alleged to be terrorists or spies," Gellman found. The Patriot

Act authorized the FBI to use these national security letters to obtain "transactional records" from financial institutions. The 2004 Intelligence Authorization Act expanded the scope of these letters beyond financial institutions to include car dealers, travel agents, real estate agents, pawnbrokers, and others. "The FBI can now obtain a vast amount of personal and highly confidential information without obtaining court approval, and without any other independent check on the validity or scope of the inquiry," said Senator Patrick Leahy of Vermont. "The privacy rights of all Americans have been compromised."

The Justice Department is churning out these national security letters. "The FBI now issues more than 30,000 National Security Letters a year," Gellman reported. And those who receive them are gagged; they are prohibited from discussing them or even the fact that they received them.

But it's not only the Justice Department that is issuing these letters. The Pentagon and the CIA have also gotten into the act. On January 14, 2007, the *New York Times* reported that the Pentagon has issued thousands of these letters, and the CIA "a handful" a year.

9. Signing Statements

The founders of our country tried to safeguard our freedoms not only by enshrining the Bill of Rights, but by constructing a system of checks and balances so that no single branch of government could tyrannize the public.

Bush has assaulted that system by issuing more than 750 "signing statements" on selected bills. Instead of vetoing legislation—which he did not do once in his first five years in office—he essentially appended an asterisk when he signed them: he would enforce them only to the extent that he believes they are constitutional, usually meaning that they don't interfere with his powers as commander in chief. "In his signing statements, Bush has repeatedly asserted that the Constitution gives him the right to ignore numerous sections of the bills—sometimes including provisions that were the subject of negotiations with Congress in order to get lawmakers to pass the bill," wrote Charlie Savage in the *Boston Globe*, in his pathbreaking story of April 30, 2006. "He has appended such statements to more than one of every ten bills he has signed," including the Patriot Act. While presidents before him have issued signing statements, Bush has done so much more than any other. Bill Clinton, for instance, issued 140 signing statements in his eight years in office. Bush, by contrast, is on a pace to issue almost ten times as many, and to use them in a way to aggrandize his own power.

"It's a challenge to the plain language of the Constitution," said Senator Arlen Specter, then chairman of the Senate Judiciary Committee, on June 27, 2006.

On December 20, 2006, Bush issued another signing statement, this one to the Postal Accountability and Enhancement Act. That act made clear, as previous laws have done, that the government does not have a right to open first-class mail without a warrant, unless there is a credible threat the piece of mail contains a bomb. But Bush in his signing statement decided to "construe" a broad exception to that, providing for "opening of an item of a class of mail otherwise sealed against inspection in a manner consistent . . . with the need to conduct searches in exigent circumstances."

10. NSA Monitoring of Your Phone Calls

President Bush's most audacious intrusion into the privacy of U.S. citizens involves his use of the National Security Agency to spy on

Americans and to mine data from their phone calls. The Foreign Intelligence Surveillance Act (FISA) states unambiguously that the "exclusive means" by which the executive branch can tap the phones of a U.S. citizen here at home is by first getting a warrant from the court it established. But Bush has refused to do that in many cases. Shortly after 9/11, and in intervals of forty-five days, he has signed an executive order authorizing the NSA to eavesdrop without a warrant on the phone calls of U.S. citizens in the United States. "The NSA is now eavesdropping on as many as 500 people in the United States at any given time, and it potentially has access to the phone calls and e-mails of millions more," James Risen wrote in *State of War*. "It does this without court-approved search warrants and with little independent oversight."

The NSA is also collecting data on two hundred million citizens by working hand in glove with AT&T, *USA Today* reported on May 10, 2006. The NSA's goal is to "create a database of every call ever made" within the nation's borders, a source told the paper, calling it "the largest database ever assembled in the world."

When the phone data-mining scandal broke, Bush said: "The privacy of ordinary Americans is fiercely protected in all our activities."

Fiercely?

On January 17, 2007, the Bush administration abruptly announced that it was ending its practice of eavesdropping without FISA warrants. Attorney General Alberto Gonzales wrote a letter to Senators Patrick Leahy and Arlen Specter of the Senate Judiciary Committee advising them that "any electronic surveillance that was occurring as part of the Terrorist Surveillance Program will now be conducted subject to the approval of the Foreign Intelligence Surveillance Court." Nevertheless, he insisted that the past practice fully complied with the law. The next day, at a Senate Judiciary Committee hearing, he seemed less sure of that: "The truth of the matter is we looked at FISA and we all concluded there's no way we can do what we have to do to protect this country under the strict reading of FISA."

11. Unconfidential Financial Records

On June 23, 2006, the Pulitzer Prize–winning team of Eric Lichtblau and James Risen of the *New York Times* revealed that the government has "examined transactions involving thousands of Americans." For doing so, they (and the editor and publisher of the *Times*) were excoriated. "Disgraceful," said Bush. "That offends me," said Cheney. "Treasonous," bellowed Representative Peter King of New York, who urged Attorney General Alberto Gonzales to prosecute. One right-wing pundit said the *Times* men should be shot by firing squad.

But what the story showed was that the government may be grabbing your financial data illegally.

The Right to Financial Privacy Act of 1978 says:

> No Government authority may have access to, or obtain copies of, the information contained in the financial records of any customer from a financial institution unless the financial records are reasonably described, [and] a copy of the subpoena or summons has been served upon the customer or mailed to his last known address.

The government can delay notice to the customer "by order of an appropriate court." There is an exception for a "legitimate law enforcement inquiry respecting name, address, account number, and type of account of particular customers."

But, according to the *Times* article, "Treasury officials did not seek individual court-approved warrants or subpoenas to examine

specific transactions, instead relying on broad administrative subpoenas for millions of records." Nor do any of the customers appear to
have been notified, and nor does the government appear to have gone
to a judge to delay that notification.

12. The Military Commissions Act

We lost a big chunk of our democracy on September 28, 2006. That
was the day the Senate voted, 65 to 34, to approve the Military Commissions Act, ensuring that this "flagrantly unconstitutional" bill, as
Senator Leahy accurately labeled it, would become law. The House
had already passed it, by a lopsided margin, and President Bush glee-
fully signed it.

This law skews our system of checks and balances. It eviscerates
the Fourth, Fifth, and Sixth Amendments. And it repudiates the
Magna Carta. It allows the president of the United States to label
anyone—including a U.S. citizen—an enemy combatant, and to deprive that person of basic due process rights to challenge his or her detention in court. And it authorizes the president "to try alien unlawful
enemy combatants" before a military tribunal, with inferior legal safe-
guards. If convicted of a serious crime in such a kangaroo court these
enemy combatants can then be executed.

This law destroys the writ of habeas corpus, the guarantee that
you can challenge your detention in court. Article I of the Constitution deals with the powers of Congress. And in Section 9 of that article, the following appears: "The privilege of the writ of habeas corpus
shall not be suspended, unless when in cases of rebellion or invasion
the public safety may require it." Thomas Jefferson once said, "Habeas
corpus secures every man here, alien or citizen, against everything

which is not law, whatever shape it may assume." But neither alien nor citizen is secure today.

"What this bill will do is take our civilization back nine hundred years," said Senator Arlen Specter, Republican of Pennsylvania, who introduced an amendment to preserve habeas corpus. That amendment failed 51–48, and then Specter turned around and voted for the bill.

At a Senate Judiciary Hearing on January 18, 2007, Specter asked Gonzales about habeas corpus. The attorney general made the following astonishing statement: "There is no express grant of habeas in the Constitution. There is a prohibition against taking it away. . . . The Constitution doesn't say every individual in the United States, or every citizen, is hereby granted or assured the right to habeas."

Gonzales went so far out on a shaky legal limb because the Military Commissions Act strips enemy combatants who are not citizens of habeas corpus. And he laid the groundwork for stripping citizens of that right as well.

The act defines an enemy combatant as "a person who has engaged in hostilities or who has purposefully and materially supported hostilities against the United States," or anyone who "has been determined to be an unlawful enemy combatant" by a tribunal set up by the president or the secretary of defense. This extraordinarily broad definition is not limited to noncitizens.

As the Center for Constitutional Rights has noted, this could mean that even lawyers for detainees at Guantánamo could be designated as enemy combatants, since they could be construed as giving "material support" to those engaged in hostilities against the United States. This law, says Vincent Warren, executive director of the center, gives the president "the privilege of kings."

The law also dilutes Common Article 3 of the Geneva Conventions in two ways. First, it outlaws violence against detainees only when that violence is "specifically intended to inflict severe physical or mental pain or suffering." Same with "cruel or inhuman treatment": it must be "intended to inflict severe or serious physical or mental pain or suffering." The law then defines "serious physical pain or suffering" as an injury that involves "substantial risk of death, extreme physical pain, a burn or physical disfigurement of a serious nature [and] significant loss or impairment of the function of a bodily member, organ, or mental faculty." Note the qualifiers: "substantial," "extreme," "serious," and "significant." They give plenty of leeway.

The new act also violates Common Article 3's requirement that detainees be afforded "all the judicial guarantees which are recognized as indispensable by civilized peoples." The passage of this law indicates that we are not a civilized people, for the Military Commissions Act does not provide those judicial guarantees: it authorizes the military tribunals to allow secret and hearsay evidence and coerced testimony.

An "alien unlawful enemy combatant," once convicted, can then be sent abroad to a penal institution of any U.S. ally, the law states. Given many detainees' experiences of extraordinary renditions, and the tortures they received at the hands of foreign governments, this little clause has not gotten the attention it deserves.

One last thing: the Military Commissions Act retroactively grants immunity to Bush administration officials who countenanced torture. Bush and Cheney and Donald Rumsfeld and Alberto Gonzales thus gave themselves, as the ACLU notes, a "get out of jail free" card for their previous actions.

Historians looking back on our era will describe the USA Patriot Act and the Military Commissions Act as bookends on the shelf marked "Assault on Democracy."

Long after George W. Bush has left office the edifice of repression that he has constructed will remain standing. Unless Congress or the courts dismantle it, some future president, at a time of real or confected crisis, will have vast powers at his disposal, powers that render our civil liberties meaningless and that mock our cherished concept of American democracy.

II

The Knock on the Door

1. *"You Have No Rights"*—*Yasser Ebrahim and Hany Ibrahim*

Yasser Ebrahim and Hany Ibrahim are brothers from Egypt. Yasser spent a lot of time in the United States between 1992 and 2001. In fact, for a while there he was married to a U.S. citizen and was living in Queens. Hany came to the United States in 1998 on a tourist visa. Yasser returned on such a visa in January 2001, and they lived together in a Brooklyn apartment with some friends even after their visas expired.

It was about 2:00 P.M. on Sunday, September 30, 2001, when their lives took a terrible turn.

They heard a knock on the door, and Yasser opened it. A dozen men were there. They were from the FBI, the INS, and the NYPD.

Yasser let them in.

The officials didn't read them their rights. They just cut to the chase and asked the brothers about 9/11 and any involvement they might have had in it—or in any terrorist activity.

Law enforcement then arrested and handcuffed Yasser and Hany and another roommate, who weren't allowed to call a lawyer. At first Yasser and Hany were taken to a holding facility on Varick Street in

Manhattan. They remained there for about twenty-four hours, during which they weren't even allowed to go to the bathroom.

(The details in this chapter are taken from a lawsuit, *Turkmen v. Ashcroft*, filed by the Center for Constitutional Rights. Yasser and Hany are plaintiffs in that suit.)

Things got worse when they were taken to the Metropolitan Detention Center in Brooklyn.

As soon as he arrived, Hany got the treatment.

Guards slammed his face into an entranceway wall that had an American flag taped to it. They called him a "motherfucker" and told him to look at the flag. They also slammed Yasser's face into the wall so hard he thought his nose was broken.

On the way up to the Administrative Maximum Special Housing Unit (the highest-security area of the facility), the guards repeatedly pushed them into walls and doors. They made Hany's handcuffs so tight that "his wrists bled," the lawsuit says. And when Hany "was ordered to walk, guards would step on his leg chains, causing him to fall. When he fell, guards would pick him up and drag him by his cuffs or clothing, then stepping on his leg chains again and repeating the process."

Yasser, too, was tripped and dragged.

And guards verbally abused them all the while, calling them "fucking Muslims" and "terrorists." The mistreatment continued, and included interference with the practice of their religion. At one point Yasser asked a counselor at the Metropolitan Detention Center about whether they had any human rights. "Forget about human rights," the counselor told him. "Three thousand people died in the World Trade Center. You have no rights."

They weren't brought before an immigration judge for five weeks.

The next time they saw a judge, on November 20, 2001, they accepted deportation orders. They were "assured that they would be removed from the country within four to five days." But that wasn't to be. They had to endure many more months of detention.

And the government knew they weren't terrorists. On December 7, 2001, FBI agents wrote up memos clearing them both for deportation. But they were forced to remain at the Metropolitan Detention Center for six months after that. They were never charged with a crime.

Hany was deported back to Egypt on May 29, 2002, Yasser on June 6, 2002. They came back to the United States for their class-action lawsuit against then attorney general John Ashcroft, FBI director Robert Mueller, James W. Ziglar, who was heading up the INS, and the warden and other correctional officers and employees at the Metropolitan Detention Center.

The Center for Constitutional Rights filed that class-action lawsuit on behalf of "male non-citizens from the Middle East, South Asia, and elsewhere who are Arab or Muslim or have been perceived by Defendants to be Arab or Muslim, who have been arrested and detained on minor immigration violations" after 9/11. The suit charges that their First, Fourth, Fifth, and Sixth Amendment rights were violated. On June 14, 2006, District Judge John Gleeson dismissed the plaintiffs' claims, except those relating to the conditions of their confinement.

"I am very disappointed and shocked," Yasser said. "I can't believe the court would allow this to happen. I am frightened for other Muslims in the United States, who could face the same discrimination and abuse that I suffered."

2. *"If This Is a Sleeper Cell, He's Comatose"—Omar Falfal*

Three times, FBI agents have knocked on Omar Falfal's door. They've never had a warrant, he says.

Born and raised in Libya, Falfal became a permanent U.S. resident in 1979 and a U.S. citizen in 1989. He lives in Lompoc, California, with his son.

The first time the agents came was three days after 9/11, he recalls. "My son opened the gate. Two agents said, 'We are FBI. We want to talk with your dad.'" Falfal let them into the kitchen. "The first question they asked me was, 'Have I been to New York?' and I said, 'Yes, in '74.' Then the second question they asked was, 'Have you been to the Twin Towers?' I said no. They also asked, 'Have you had anybody living with you who passed away recently?'" Falfal said no to that as well, and they began to pry further, he says.

"What religion are you?"

"I'm a Muslim."

"Sunni or Shiite?"

"I'm a Sunni."

After that they asked about his marital status (divorced), and his occupation (Falfal is disabled, with three blood clots in his leg). The interview ended pleasantly enough.

"I promised them I'd be an excellent citizen," he recalls. "I told them: 'I entered this country clean. I will leave this country cleaner. No harm will come from this body.'" The next time he heard from the FBI was in April 2002, when an agent called him on the phone. That was only a brief conversation, with the agent telling Falfal he wanted to talk to him again. It took awhile, but three years later, in April 2005, the FBI was back at his house.

"I was cutting the grass" when they showed up, he says.

They asked him about an acquaintance of his. "We don't want to see anyone having a belt around their waist," one agent told him, making an allusion to a suicide bomber.

"I told them, 'The gentleman you mentioned is one of the cleanest and nicest people in the world. His mom was a school principal in the 1960s in Libya. He had a master's degree. He's known not to cause any trouble. The man loves America, he talks nice about America, you should divert your resources to a real threat. He's not that type.'" Falfal said they then asked him about the imam at the local Islamic center.

"I said, 'The imam's a really nice man. He gathers Muslims, Christians, and Jews together.'"

They had one final question, a political one, Falfal recalls. "What do you think of the conflict between Israel and the Palestinians?"

"I was going to say 'I'm not the U.S. ambassador to the United Nations,' but I told them this: 'The United States should be fair to both parties, neutral, and for both the Palestinians and Israelis, they should have their own homelands and be respectful of each other and not harm one another.'"

A couple of months later, he received a letter notifying him that his phone had been tapped that spring. "To be honest with you, I was scared. I've had no misdemeanors, no traffic violations. I've never done anything wrong."

Falfal decided to move. He'd had enough of the FBI visits, and he was sick of his neighbor, who kept calling him a terrorist. But the FBI came to his next home. On March 22, 2006, at about ten in the morning, they knocked on the door. "I cut the questions short this time," he says. "I said, 'I'd be happy to speak with you, but I need the assistance of my attorney.' They accepted that." Falfal didn't even have an attorney at the time. "But I didn't know what to do. Are they going to grab me or take me off to prison? You never know what they're going to do." Within ten days, the Arab-American Anti-Discrimination Com-

mittee had found him an attorney, Mark Allen Kleiman. When Falfal
tells me this he begins to cry, so grateful is he for the assistance
Kleiman has provided him.

"I immediately called the agents who had asked for another interview," says Kleiman. "Neither of us have heard from them since. I felt
the FBI needed a chaperone. I guess they don't want to go to the
prom." Kleiman says Falfal "is less interested in politics than just
about anyone else I've met who has caught the FBI's attention in decades. If this is a sleeper cell, he's comatose." He objects to the fact that
Falfal was asked about his religion. And he says Falfal's views of the
Palestinian-Israeli conflict should not be held against him. "If that's a
criterion for being investigated, there are members of Congress
whose heads are on the block." He has filed Freedom of Information
Act requests with the FBI about Falfal. "The next step is a civil rights
complaint against the bureau," he says.

"It's certainly not uncommon for agents to visit individuals when
gathering information," says Laura Eimiller, spokesperson for the FBI
in Los Angeles. "I'm not familiar with this individual, and I'm not at
liberty to comment on interviews that are conducted." Falfal believes
he's been treated unfairly. "For being a U.S. citizen, for being in a country that stands for democracy, and freedom, and rights, I didn't see any
of that. I see nothing but abuse."

3. *"I Was Just Getting a Cup of Coffee"—Marc Schultz*

Marc Schultz just wanted to get a cup of coffee before a big day at
work. It was Saturday, June 21, 2003, and he was employed at Chapter
11 Discount Books in Atlanta. He was bracing himself for a rush, since
it was the day a new Harry Potter book was coming out.

While standing in line at a Caribou Coffee shop he read an article his father had printed off the Web for him. That article, from the *Weekly Planet* of Tampa, was called "Weapons of Mass Stupidity: Fox News Hits a New Lowest Common Denominator." Another customer at Caribou Coffee evidently saw Schultz reading the article and called the FBI on him.

On June 24, two FBI agents visited Schultz, then twenty-five, at the bookstore.

He wrote all about it in an eye-opening article for *Creative Loafing Atlanta*: " 'You Marc Schultz?' asks the tall one. He shows me his badge, introduces himself as Special Agent Clay Trippi. . . . 'Do you drive a black Nissan Altima?' " Agent Trippi asks him if he was at the Caribou Coffee on Powers Ferry in Atlanta that Saturday morning. Schultz says yes. Then they ask him what he was carrying into the store.

"Trippi's partner speaks up: 'Any reading material? Papers?' . . . Then Trippi decides to level with me: 'I'll tell you what, Marc. Someone in the shop that day saw you reading something, and thought it looked suspicious enough to call us about. So that's why we're here, just checking it out. Like I said, there's no problem. We'd just like to get to the bottom of this. Now if we can't, then you might have a problem. And you don't want that.' "

Schultz tells them it was "some kind of left-wing editorial," but he can't recall the exact article. The agents press him for the details: author, title, what it was about. After they leave Schultz remembers the "Weapons of Mass Stupidity" story, so he calls the FBI and leaves the details on a phone-answering machine.

Joe Parris, media coordinator for the FBI's Atlanta office, "wouldn't confirm or deny the Schultz interview," *Creative Loafing* reported. But Parris did say, "In this post-9/11 era, it is the absolute responsibility of the FBI to follow through on any tips of potential terrorist activity. Are people going to take exception and be inconvenienced by this at times? Oh, yeah. . . . A certain amount of convenience is going to be offset by an increase in security." I followed up with both Schultz and Parris.

Schultz says, "It just seems so perplexing. My main question is what the FBI thought this document was that constituted such a problem."

Parris says, "As I've explained to *Creative Loafing* ad nauseam, I can't specifically comment on this particular case even to acknowledge that it's happened. Everybody wants to turn this into a thought-police story. But any time a citizen calls up with a suspicion of terrorist activity, we have no choice but to follow up on it. We have to err on the side of talking to too many people, because God help us if we don't talk to the next Mohammed Atta. . . . We don't go out and interview people for what they read. Portraying any incident as us doing this sells the organization short, and it undermines the public trust."

For Schultz, the incident confirms some of his worst fears. "I'm very liberal," he says, "and sometimes my friends say I'm giving them some kind of paranoid, nutty stuff, but then the FBI shows up."

4. All They Wanted Was Training in Disaster Relief— *Yaju Dharmarajah and Pilar Schiavo*

Yaju Dharmarajah and his wife, Pilar Schiavo, were living in Hadley, Massachusetts, and hoping to do international refugee work. They had taken trainings with the International Red Cross, and they wanted a few more. So on July 3, 2002, Dharmarajah called the Massachusetts Emergency Management Agency (MEMA) and left a message to see if they could participate in one of its training sessions.

"I got a call back on July 5," he says. "An outreach director asked why we were interested in trainings. We told her we wanted to do refugee and relief work in Africa and Asia. Then she said, 'What do you do for a living?'

"I said, 'I'm a union organizer, and my wife is a documentary filmmaker.' Then she asked me again why I wanted to get training." The whole conversation lasted only two minutes or so.

Five days later, on July 10, an Amherst police officer and a University of Massachusetts–Amherst police officer came calling. Both were in plainclothes, the couple says. The Amherst police officer was Sergeant Charles H. Nelson, who left his card. Dharmarajah and Schiavo believe the UMass officer was Barry Flanders, who was also working with the FBI.

"It was early afternoon, maybe like two or three, and they knocked," says Schiavo, who was born in the United States. "I thought it was the neighbor, and I just yelled, 'Come in.' Then I heard these male voices, and I said, 'Oh, just a minute.' They said they were looking for a Pilar and a Yaju. I said, 'I'm Pilar.' And they said, 'We got a call from MEMA, and we want to ask you a couple of questions.'

"I didn't allow them in. I was talking through the screen. At first I couldn't think who MEMA was, and then I said, 'OK.' They said, 'We got a call from them saying you were interested in trainings on terrorism and you wanted to film them.' I kind of laughed, and I said, 'I didn't want to film them, and we didn't call them about trainings in terrorism. That has nothing to do with what we're interested in. We wanted training on disaster relief.'

"They asked why. I said, 'We're wanting to do refugee work, and we're trying to build our résumés.' They asked me what my films were about. I told them: One is about a woman on the men's wrestling team in high school, and another is about three gay men in a white community, and the other is about community organizing on low-wage work.

"One of the officers asked if we were affiliated with any organizations. I said, 'No, I was in the room when my husband made this phone call, and he didn't say anything about terrorism. I think someone's projecting their own fears.' One of them said, 'Yeah, that could be. We've been getting a lot of calls with everything going on.' "

For Schiavo and Dharmarajah, the visit was rattling.

"It's just very scary," says Schiavo. "We were a little nervous about speaking out about it. People aren't thinking with reason right now." They suspect that their phone has been tapped.

"We don't know if we're on a list now," Schiavo says. "We had been hoping to go to Montreal, but now we're afraid to cross the border, because he could be detained indefinitely. And we're worried about applying for jobs now. We wonder if we're damaged goods and we won't be able to get international work just because the woman my husband talked to at MEMA was paranoid about his accent."

A spokesperson for MEMA was not able to track down any information on this case, and the FBI in Boston had no comment. Neither Sergeant Nelson nor Officer Flanders returned phone calls seeking comment.

Dharmarajah is a Tamil, a member of a persecuted minority in Sri Lanka, and he says this experience brought a sense of déjà vu. "We were used to being pulled out of cars and put into jail," he says. "It happened to the entire family. They'd do raids on our house and put us in jail for a day, or a couple of hours, and then we'd get out." He acknowledges that the repression in the United States is nowhere near what it was like in Sri Lanka, but says he remains on edge. "Because of the Patriot Act, we have no rights. I can be deported, and I can be held without charges, and my wife has no way of knowing where I am."

5. Homeland Security Opens the Mail—Grant Goodman

Grant Goodman is an eighty-one-year-old emeritus professor of Asian history at the University of Kansas. He has had an ongoing correspondence by snail mail with a former professor of history at the University of the Philippines, where Goodman had taught on three separate occasions. In early December 2005, he was shocked when a letter arrived from her that had already been opened.

"The bottom of the envelope had been slashed open and then retaped with green tape," says Goodman. "And it said, 'Opened by Border Protection' in great big letters. The U.S. Department of Homeland Security seal is on it, too." Goodman believes his rights have "absolutely" been violated. "I just couldn't believe it, and wondered what in the world is going on." This story was broken by Joel Mathis of the *Lawrence Journal-World*. A Department of Homeland Security spokesman told the *Journal-World* that "he didn't know how often the agency opened mail from abroad. And he wouldn't discuss the criteria for opening letters."

Goodman worries that he "must be under surveillance for one reason or other." He won't release the name of the former professor in the Philippines, but says she is in her mid-eighties and hardly a security risk. "This is a very devout Catholic woman who goes to six o'clock mass every evening, and I don't know what they would be interested in her for," he says. "She hasn't written about anything in years."

He hopes that his disclosure of this mail tampering will encourage other people to expose similar invasions of privacy. "I purposely gave the letter to the newspaper in hopes that others would come forward with their experiences, but none have so far." He is amazed at the crudeness of Homeland Security. In his historical research he saw many better examples. "I know how the Japanese opened mail," he says. "In the 1930s they were very good at it. The people whose mail they were reading didn't even know they had opened it."

6. *Gagged Library Exec Speaks Out—George Christian*

George Christian was the executive director of Library Connection, a nonprofit cooperative of more than two dozen public and academic libraries in Connecticut, in the summer of 2005 when his office received an odd call. It wasn't from a co-op member. And it wasn't from a library patron. It was from the FBI.

One of Christian's staff answered the phone and then brought him the news.

" 'We got a call from the FBI, they want to send us something called a "national security letter," and they asked who to address it to, and I told them you,' " the staffer informed him. "I thought, national security what? What's a national security letter? Until that moment I'd never heard those three words, national security letter. I never knew there was such a thing. I had no inkling whatsoever," Christian says.

He says the phone call alerting him that he was about to get such a letter gave him enough time to research the issue and to decide that "this was not something I wanted to cooperate with." He says he was torn. "On the one hand, I think I'm a good citizen. Certainly, the average citizen would want to cooperate. Half of me was saying, help your country out. But in the back of my mind I was thinking, wait a minute, these aren't the rules this country was founded on."

When two FBI agents showed up at his office and handed him the national security letter, he told them why he objected. He says they didn't demand the information on the spot, "so we politely parted company."

That specific letter, according to Barton Gellman of the *Washing-ton Post*, sought "all subscriber information, billing information, and access logs of any person" who used a specific computer at a nearby library.

While Christian says he wasn't scared by the FBI encounter, he wasn't ecstatic, either. "The first intimidating thing was the fact that this letter made really clear that I could discuss receipt of this letter with no one," he says. "And the second thing was the good cop, bad cop routine. One FBI agent was professionally dressed, in a coat and tie, and was mild-mannered, and the other one was casually dressed and muscular and didn't speak much at all." He contacted an attorney who had worked with his organization before, and she directed him to the ACLU, which was glad to take his case and that of the three librarians on his executive board: Barbara Bailey, Peter Chase, and Janet Nocek. (Chase, by the way, is chairman of the intellectual freedom committee of the Connecticut Library Association.) The four plaintiffs were not allowed even to enter the courtroom in Bridgeport, Connecticut, when their case was first heard for fear that their identities as the re-cipients of the letter would be obvious. Judge Janet Hall arranged for the four to watch the proceedings by remote from the federal district court in Hartford, about sixty miles away.

Christian and his colleagues were suing on two grounds: to de-clare the national security letter unconstitutional, and to lift the gag order so that they could at least publicly acknowledge that they had been hit by such a letter.

In fall 2006, Judge Hall ruled in their favor on the gag order, in part because news outlets had already identified the group as a result of the government's own sloppiness in redacting documents. How-ever, Judge Hall stayed her decision upon the government's request for appeal. Christian said the gag was particularly painful at that time, because he wanted to testify before Congress, which was then debating renewing the Patriot Act.

But the government dragged out the appeal until after Congress renewed the Patriot Act. This rankles Christian. "They were really happy to have us gagged while the debate was going on in Congress. As soon as that was over, although our circumstances hadn't changed, suddenly they said there's no point in continuing the gag anyway. Clearly, here they were trying to keep me from going before Congress. That's like allowing me to call the fire department only after the building has burned to the ground."

Chase feels the same way. "The government was telling Congress that it didn't use the Patriot Act against libraries and that no one's rights had been violated," he said in an ACLU press statement. "I felt that I just could not be part of this fraud being foisted on our nation."

"Our clients were gagged by the government at a time when Congress needed to hear their voices the most," added Ann Beeson, the ACLU's associate legal director, in that press release. "This Administration has repeatedly shown that it will hide behind the cloak of national security to silence its critics and cover up embarrassing facts."

Even today Christian and his colleagues are not free to discuss the content of the national security letter. "We can now say that our organization was the recipient of a national security letter, and that the letter requested library records," he says. "But that's it. We can't tell you when we got the letter, we can't tell you who signed it, we can't tell you what the letter requested us to turn over. I can't get into anything." He does not, by any means, believe he has compromised national security by not cooperating with the FBI. "I have no worry whatsoever. Because if it was really that important the FBI could have gone at any time before a judge and said, 'Here's the evidence. We want a warrant.' They never did that. So I don't lose any sleep over it."

Christian believes that "the situation is getting out of hand" when the government issues thirty thousand national security letters a year. "If you don't count Sundays, that's about one hundred a day," he says. "And there's no evidence they're apprehending one hundred potential terrorists a day—or even one a day."

III

Repression and Infiltration

1. *"A Disgrace for the Community"—Welcome to Miami*

It's not every day that a sitting judge alleges that he saw the police commit felonies. But that's what Circuit Judge Richard Margolius said on December 11, 2003, regarding police misconduct in Miami during the protests against the Free Trade Area of the Americas agreement (FTAA) in late November of that year.

Judge Margolius was presiding over a case that the protesters had brought against the city. He said he saw the police commit at least twenty felonies, Amy Driscoll of the *Miami Herald* reported. "Pretty disgraceful what I saw with my own eyes," he said, according to the paper. "This was a real eye-opener. A disgrace for the community."

Police used tasers, shock batons, rubber bullets, beanbags filled with chemicals, large sticks, and concussion grenades against lawful protesters. (Just prior to the FTAA protests the city of Miami had passed an ordinance requiring a permit for any gathering of more than six people for longer than twenty-nine minutes.) Police took the offensive, wading into crowds and pursuing the demonstrators. They arrested more than 250 protesters. Almost all of them were simply exercising their First Amendment rights. Police also seized protest material and destroyed it, and they confiscated personal property, demonstrators say.

"How many police officers have been charged by the state attorney so far for what happened out there during the FTAA?" the judge asked in court, according to the *Herald*. The prosecutor said none. "Pretty sad commentary, at least from what I saw," the judge retorted.

Even for veterans of protests, the police actions in Miami were unlike any they had encountered before. "I've been to a number of the antiglobalization protests—Seattle, Cancún, D.C.—and this was different," says Norm Stockwell, operations coordinator for WORT, the community radio station in Madison, Wisconsin. "At previous events the police force was defensive. In Miami the police were poised to go after the protesters, and that's what they did. They actually went into the crowds to divide the protesters, then chased them into different neighborhoods."

He says some reporters also were mistreated, especially if they were not "embedded" with the Miami police. "I got shot twice [with rubber projectiles], once in the back, another time in the leg," reports Jeremy Scahill of *Democracy Now!* "John Hamilton from the Workers Independent News Service was shot in the neck by a pepper-spray pellet." Ana Nogueira, Scahill's colleague from *Democracy Now!*, was videotaping some of the police mayhem when she was arrested. "In police custody the authorities made Ana remove her clothes, because they were pepper sprayed. The police forced her to strip naked in front of male officers."

John Heckenlively, former head of the Racine County Democratic Party in Wisconsin, says he was cornered by the Miami police late in the afternoon of November 20. He and a few companions had been trying to move away from the protest area when "a large cordon of police, filling the entire block edge to edge, was moving up the street. As they approached, an officer told us that we should leave the area. We informed him that was precisely what we were attempting to do, and seconds later, he placed us under arrest." Police kept Heckenlively in tight handcuffs behind his back for more than six hours, he says, adding that he was held for a total of sixty hours.

Trade unionists were particularly outraged at the treatment they received in Miami. John Sweeney, head of the AFL-CIO, wrote then attorney general John Ashcroft on December 3 to urge the Justice Department to investigate "the massive and unwarranted repression of constitutional rights and civil liberties that took place in Miami." He wrote that on November 20, police interfered with the federation's demonstration "by denying access to buses, blocking access to the amphitheater where the rally was occurring, and deploying armored personnel carriers, water cannons, and scores of police in riot gear with clubs in front of the amphitheater entrance. Some union retirees had their buses turned away from Miami altogether by the police, and were sent back home."

Blocking access to the rally was the least of it, Sweeney wrote. After the march "police advanced on groups of peaceful protesters without provocation. The police failed to provide those in the crowd with a safe route to disperse, and then deployed pepper spray and rubber bullets against protesters as they tried to leave the scene. Along with the other peaceful protesters, AFL-CIO staff, union peacekeepers, and retirees were trapped in the police advance. One retiree sitting on a chair was sprayed directly in the face with pepper spray. An AFL-CIO staff member was hit by a rubber bullet while trying to leave the scene. When the wife of a retired steelworker verbally protested police tactics, she was thrown to the ground on her face and a gun was pointed to her head."

The ACLU of Greater Miami has filed several lawsuits against the

city over its FTAA actions, including one on behalf of the trade unionists and one on behalf of Edward Owaki, a University of Massachusetts student.

Owaki "was viciously attacked by police," that lawsuit says. While
at the FTAA protest and acting peacefully, Owaki "was struck from
behind on the head three times with a three-foot-long wooden baton,
swung in an overhand motion" by a police officer. He was then handcuffed and taken to the hospital, where he was given just Tylenol, and
after ten minutes the police incarcerated him at the Miami Dade
County Jail. When he was released the next day he was placed in in-
tensive care, and "was treated for symptoms including a skull frac-
ture, cerebral contusions, epidural hematoma, epidural hemorrhage,
slurred speech, dizziness, vomiting, loss of consciousness, and
seizure." He was in the hospital for nine days.

"This was a clear abuse of power by the police, and an indiscriminate use of force," says Lida Rodriguez-Taseff, then president of the
ACLU of Greater Miami. "People who were retreating were being
shot in the back with rubber bullets. . . . Carl Kesser was filming the
police, and he was hit in the head with a beanbag above his eye socket.
If it had hit him a little bit lower he could have lost his eye. The police
were using tasers on people who were down, who were already re-
strained. These police officers were using these weapons as if they
were Pez dispensers. They acted like, as long as it wasn't a firearm,
they could use the weapons to their hearts' content."

"We did what we had to do based on the situation at the time," says
Miami police officer Herminia Salas-Jacobson. "If anyone has any concerns or questions, we've asked them to come forward, and we will address each one one on an individual basis."

To fund the police operation the force used $8.5 million of an $87
billion appropriation Congress had passed for Iraq reconstruction.
Police Chief John Timoney thanked his officers for their "remarkable

restraint." And he won praise in some law enforcement quarters for what is being called the Miami model. "The 'Miami model' was a police tactic designed to intimidate political demonstrators, silence dissent, and criminalize protest against the government policies," says Terry Coble, president of the ACLU of Greater Miami. "If this type of police action is allowed to continue, our country will have lost one of our most basic rights, and we will be on the road to a totalitarian government."

2. An Olympic Experience in Utah—Music Group Pulled Over at Gunpoint: "What Ethnic Groups Are Onboard?"

On February 13, 2002, during the winter games, a musical group called Alma Melodioso had an Olympic experience. The California-based band, which plays Latin styles of music, was on its way from Monroe, Utah, to a gig at the Olympic Plaza in Park City.

"Before we got to Provo we had stopped at a convenience store," recalls drummer Bob Sanders. "While we were in the store I asked the clerk if he knew about security checkpoints on the way to the Olympics, because we were running late and were worried about traffic being backed up." The clerk didn't know.

Some other people from the group were in the store, and the TV was on, and a report aired about U.S. planning to attack Iraq. "I can't believe we're going to do this," said one of the members, denouncing Bush's war on terror, according to Sanders. The band members, nine in all, got back on their old, renovated school bus.

"About another ten minutes down the road, a cop car got up right behind us, and then another one. They piled up about five cop cars behind us, and one in front of us, and they flashed us to follow them. They pulled us off onto the exit ramp just outside of Provo, and basically they shut off the whole ramp and barricaded it with their cars. They had cops in front of us, in back of us, and up on the highway and in the field. We were completely surrounded." He says they had no idea why they were being pulled over. One police officer told the driver, Felicity Morton, to come out with her hands up. "They had their guns out," Sanders says. They started asking her questions like: "What are you doing in Utah?" and "Have you done anything that might have raised suspicion at that last stop you were at?" And then they asked, "What ethnic groups are onboard the bus?"

Morton told them, "We're just white American people, except Noella, who looks Mexican but is from California." When they were talking with Morton the head highway patrolman asked if he could come on the bus. "We said yeah," Sanders says. Then the patrolman said, "There's some things you did that caused some suspicion."

"It dawned on me right then," says Sanders. "I told them I had asked about security checkpoints. And they said, 'Yes, that's what this was about.' "

The patrolman ran all of their IDs through the computer. Then a couple of FBI agents showed up "dressed as ski bunnies," Sanders says, and then Secret Service agents arrived and came on the bus and started searching it. "They went through our backpacks and purses. Then one Secret Service agent asked, 'Who's Bob Sanders?' I kind of went, 'Whoa, why are they interested in me?' "

"I found some things in your backpack that are concerning me," the agent said, according to Sanders. "Do you know what that might be? Let's take a look." Sanders was ordered to open his backpack. At that point he saw some *San Francisco Chronicle* articles a friend had given him that expressed opinions against the war in Afghanistan and the war on terrorism.

" 'That's what I'm concerned about,' she said. She started asking me about where I had gotten these articles, and why was I interested in these issues, and where I had first gotten interested in politics, and where I formed the political beliefs that I had. And then she wanted to know other things, like do I ever go watch political speakers, like congressmen or the president, or former presidents, or do I ever visit political [Web] sites.

"I just told her that I've always kind of been a curious person, and always have been interested in politics, and that in college I was turned on by professors to ideas that weren't exactly mainstream. But as far as seeing presidents or visiting political [Web] sites, I said I never do any of that stuff."

Then she said, "OK, thank you," and that was it.

The Utah Highway Patrol and the Secret Service did not return phone calls on this story. But highway patrol spokesman Doug McCleve told the *Deseret News* on February 14, "Because we're in a heightened state of alert, we reacted, issued an all-points alert, located the bus, and closed down the freeway ramp until we could investigate. We have an obligation to the public to be very, very responsive right now."

Special Agent Kevin Eaton, an FBI supervisor in Salt Lake City, told me he had checked his computers and the names of the group members "are not in there. Especially if there was nothing to it, we wouldn't have made a record."

Sanders wonders about the incident. "What if there had been someone of Middle Eastern descent in our group? Would we have seen our friend again?"

And though the FBI says it didn't make a file on the group, it had an effect. "I'm actually fearful now of having any material or speaking out against our government," Sanders told me shortly after the incident. "You cannot be critical of the government right now. If you're not patriotic or a nationalist you could be singled out."

3. National Guard, Pentagon Peep at Raging Grannies

The Mother's Day action on May 8, 2005, in Sacramento was nothing too threatening. About thirty-five people attended the rally, which was co-sponsored by three peace groups: CodePink, the Peninsula Raging Grannies, and Gold Star Families for Peace, a group whose members have lost loved ones in Iraq. The protesters gathered on the grounds of the state capitol near the Vietnam War memorial and urged an end to the Iraq War.

"We wanted to commemorate the original creation of Mother's Day, dating back to the 1800s, with Julia Ward Howe's antiwar proclamation," said Natalie Wormeli, a co-founder of the Davis chapter of CodePink. Howe's proclamation, which the women read at the event, begins, "Arise, then, women of this day!" It says that women should "bewail and commemorate the dead," and it warns, "The sword of murder is not the balance of justice! Blood does not wipe out dishonor nor violence indicate possession." The proclamation urges disarmament and ends with the hope that "the great human family can live in peace."

The demonstrators wailed and sang a few songs, Wormeli says, and they also heard from Pat Sheehan, whose son Casey died in Baghdad. "My wife, Cindy, was supposed to be there but couldn't make it, and so I was just there to say a few words about my son," he recalls.

Unbeknownst to the protesters, the National Guard was monitoring their action, according to a June 26 article in the San Jose *Mercury News* by Dion Nissenbaum. "Three days before the rally, as a courtesy to the military, an aide in Governor Arnold Schwarzenegger's press office alerted the guard to the event, according to e-mails obtained by the *Mercury News*," the story said. One of those e-mails was from National Guard chief of staff Colonel John Moorman, who was writing to Major General Thomas Eres, head of the guard: "Sir, Information you wanted on Sunday's demonstration at the Capitol." Moorman copied the e-mail to other top commanders, including Colonel Jeff Davis, who oversees a new intelligence-gathering operation of the California National Guard, the paper said. Davis responded to the e-mail: "Thanks, Forwarding same to our Intell. folks who continue to monitor."

When Wormeli heard about this she was taken aback. "I was both kind of angry and sad at the same time," she says. "Angry that they would waste their time and money on this, and sad because I don't know how it would impact activists who might not want to deal with the National Guard." Pat Sheehan also denounced the apparent surveillance: "I think it's ridiculous," he told me.

Medea Benjamin, one of the founders of CodePink, said, "What has this country come to when our National Guard is off fighting in Iraq instead of home protecting us from natural disasters, and the few guardsmen and -women who are still here are assigned to investigate women who are calling for peace?"

Lieutenant Colonel Stan Zezotarski of the guard justified its interest in at least following the protest groups in the media. "Who knows who could infiltrate that type of group and try to stir something up?" he told the *Mercury News*. "After all, we live in the age of terrorism, so who knows?"

Lieutenant Colonel Douglas Hart, the director of public affairs for the guard, denies anything untoward occurred. "Let me explain to you exactly what happened," he told me. "There was a protest down at the capitol, and they have to put in a request to do this kind of protest at the capitol. And in their request they said they were going to urge the governor to bring National Guard troops back from Iraq. The governor's office forwarded that information to me, and I let my boss know, and he had our joint operations center monitor the news so he could see what was said. It's that simple."

The Raging Grannies responded in typical fashion. They put on skits outside the National Guard's armory in Redwood on July 1. And they came up with appropriate lyrics.

To the tune of "Someone to Watch over Me," they wrote the following verse:

> Schwarzenegger do you think I'm a spy?
> I know that I
> Cannot see why
> Someone would watch over me.

And they adapted the Christmas carol "Santa Claus Is Coming to Town":

> You better watch out
> You better comply
> You better not doubt
> The National Guard is all over town.

But it wasn't just the National Guard. It was the Pentagon itself that was surveilling CodePink and the Raging Grannies in Northern California, according to a Pentagon document that MSNBC obtained, which disclosed the monitoring of forty-three groups in twenty states, plus the District of Columbia. The Pentagon made notations on a November 10, 2004, protest at the Sacramento Military Entrance Processing Station ("Disposition: Open/Unresolved," the document states) and at a May 7, 2005, counterrecruiting protest at the San Francisco Recruiting Station ("probably peaceful," it notes).

"We are not the enemy of the state," says Wormeli. "And I do worry it could have a chilling effect on newcomers to the cause. I get concerned we're headed to a new COINTELPRO. The U.S. can do better this. We should not be living in a surveillance society."

(COINTELPRO refers to the 1960s and early 1970s FBI counterintelligence program, which infiltrated and disrupted dissident groups.)

Robertson of the Raging Grannies says, "I guess they still don't get it that grannies in flowery hats are peaceable." Gail Sredanovic, another co-chair of the Peninsula Raging Grannies, found the reports of spying absurd and alarming: "You have to ask who's next: the League of Women Voters? The PTA?"

4. "He Took a Lot of Notes"—An Imposter at Peace Fresno

He took a lot of notes.

That's how one member of a California antiwar group, Peace Fresno, described Aaron Kilner, a member of the Fresno County Sheriff's Department, who had infiltrated the group. (You may have seen a bit on this in Michael Moore's *Fahrenheit 9/11.*) To the activists he was known as Aaron Stokes, and he'd been attending meetings and going to events for more than six months, says Camille Russell, who was president of Peace Fresno in 2002. She and Peace Fresno realized he was an infiltrator only after he died in a motorcycle accident at the end of August 2003. "I saw an article in the *Fresno Bee*, and I saw this picture of a guy we knew as Aaron Stokes," she recalls. "But the article identified him as Aaron Kilner, a deputy sheriff working for the antiterrorism unit."

She was shocked, to say the least. "We thought he was one of us, and when we read this, we felt betrayed," says Russell, an elementary teacher. "It's a very uncomfortable feeling. When we learned he was working for the antiterrorism unit, we realized we were targeted because of our strong, vocal criticism of the Bush administration." She does not appreciate the implication that she is a terrorist. "It is scary to

think that the government would view someone who is simply involved in criticism of the government as a terrorist. We feel this is a violation of our First Amendment rights, and we want people to know
that the government is doing this kind of thing."

The sheriff's department denies it did anything wrong. "For the
purpose of detecting or preventing terrorist activities, the Fresno
County Sheriff's Department may visit any place and attend any event
that is open to the public, on the same terms and conditions as members of the public generally," says a statement the department released. "Detective Aaron Kilner was a member of the Fresno County
Sheriff's Department Anti-Terrorism unit. This unit collects, evalu-
ates, collates, analyzes, and disseminates information on individuals,
groups, and organizations suspected of criminal or terrorist activities.
This information meets the stringent federal and state guidelines for
intelligence gathering and civil rights protections in order to prevent
crime and protect the health and safety of residents of Fresno County
and the state of California." The sheriff's department says Peace
Fresno is not under investigation.

The ACLU of Northern California and Peace Fresno filed Freedom of Information Act requests with the FBI and the U.S. attorney
on January 29, 2004. The groups are seeking any and all documents
the FBI has on Peace Fresno. In addition, they are requesting any and
all documents about the "monitoring, surveillance, infiltration, or investigation of religious organizations or groups, places of worship,
community groups, demonstrations, anti-war groups, and other activist groups or individuals in California."

"Peace Fresno is a very distressed and outraged organization, and
the more they reflect on what happened to them the more distressed
and outraged they become," says Catherine Campbell, an attorney for
the antiwar group.

Even before the widespread spying on other groups became public, Campbell and Peace Fresno suspected it. "If it's happening to Peace Fresno, it's happening to others," she says. "The only reason we found out about it is because of a fluke."

5. *"Is This 1984 or What?"*—*Sarah Bardwell*

In the summer of 2004 Sarah Bardwell was a twenty-one-year-old intern at the American Friends Service Committee in Denver. Four FBI agents and two Denver police officers came to her home on July 22, at about 4:30 in the afternoon, she recalls: "One guy was in all SWAT, dressed in black, with six guns on him." They gathered Bardwell and her housemates together. "They told us they were 'doing community outreach,' but then they said they were doing 'preemptive investigations' into possible or suspected 'anarchists, terrorists, and murderers.'

"The FBI agents then began to probe about upcoming political events. They asked us if we were planning any criminal actions at the Republican National Convention, the Democratic National Convention, and the inauguration," Bardwell says. "And then they asked us if we knew anyone who was planning such actions. And they told us if we withheld this information, that was a crime." One of her housemates asked them if they had a warrant, and they responded something like this, Bardwell says: " 'Oh, we don't need a warrant. We're just here to talk. It's a friendly visit.' " There was some banter back and forth, she recalls. "They asked us what our names were. We told them they probably knew our names, but we didn't give them to them. We asked for their names, but they said they wouldn't give us theirs if we didn't give them ours."

Then the conversation turned ominous.

"They told us they were going to have to take 'more intrusive efforts' because they took the fact that we were not answering their questions as noncooperation," she says. "I asked if that was a threat. They denied that it was. And they left shortly after that, saying something like, 'We'll see you later.' And me thinking, 'I hope not.' " Looking back Bardwell recognizes how scared she was. "I was afraid the whole time, afraid of what they were going to do to my house, afraid of my safety and my future. It's a really scary thing to have the FBI say they're going to be more intrusive than coming to your house!" When the FBI left, her roommates all expressed "shock and fear and anger. 'Is this 1984 or what?' got said probably a million times."

While the FBI and Denver police were descending on Bardwell's home, another team appeared at their friends' house down the street.

The FBI denied doing anything improper. "The FBI is not monitoring groups, or interviewing individuals, unless we receive intelligence that such individuals or groups may be planning violent and disruptive criminal activity or have knowledge of such activity," said the FBI in a press release on August 16, 2004. That press release, which was in response to a *New York Times* article that had mentioned Bardwell's experience, stated in general terms that the bureau had received "information that individuals were planning to conduct violent criminal activity" during the upcoming political conventions.

"No one at the house was planning on going to the conventions," says Bardwell. "It's really weird."

An August 2, 2004, FBI memo obtained later by the ACLU said, in fact, that the agency was engaging in "pretext interviews to gain general information concerning possible criminal activity at the upcoming political conventions and Presidential elections." The ACLU also obtained a December 2004 memo that mentions Bardwell as being of interest because she was an antiwar protester and a member of Food Not Bombs, which the memo said had a "close association" with anarchists.

The Justice Department's Office of the Inspector General issued a report entitled "The FBI's Investigative Activities Concerning Potential Protesters at the 2004 Democratic and Republican National Political Conventions." The report, dated April 27, 2006, found no fault with the FBI. "Our review did not substantiate the allegations that the FBI improperly targeted protesters for interviews in an effort to chill the exercise of their First Amendment rights at the 2004 Democratic and Republican National Political Conventions," it said. "We concluded that the FBI's interviews of potential convention protesters and others that we reviewed were conducted for legitimate law enforcement purposes."

6. *Abu Ghraib Mimicker Arrested on Bogus Bomb Charge—Joe Previtera*

On May 26, 2004, Joe Previtera decided to protest the torture of Iraqi prisoners by U.S. soldiers. The twenty-one-year-old Boston College student and a few members of his antiwar group went down to the military recruitment office on Tremont Street near the Boston Commons.

Outside the Armed Forces Career Center, on the sidewalk, he stood on a milk crate. He wore a black shawl and placed a black hood over his head. And he attached stereo wires to his fingers, imitating the notorious picture of the Abu Ghraib prisoner. "We wanted to humanize this issue by having people see in person a depiction of the torture," Previtera says. He also wanted to make an impact on potential recruits: "The location was strategically picked to give people who were thinking of enlisting an alternative perspective of the military than what would be given to them by the military recruiter."

At first, the reaction was mild. "Some people were walking by thanking us," he recalls. "A group of men working next door said I should be there every day. Someone else came by and said, 'Disgusting.'" One man from the recruiting center wasn't too happy, either.

"He put his hand on my shoulder to get me off" the crate, but Previtera stayed on. After about forty-five minutes, the police showed up. "One of the police officers called me a sissy because I was putting my arms down, and he said if I was like the guy in the real picture I should keep my arms out."

Then one of Previtera's fellow protesters warned him that the police were beginning to get aggressive. "I stepped down from the milk crate and took my hood off," Previtera says. "There were four policemen right in front of me. I tried to walk away. They said, 'You can't go anywhere.' They said I had to wait because the bomb squad was coming." Previtera was not expecting this. "I couldn't believe it. I just stood there in shock." The police proceeded to arrest him.

"I asked them for what. And they said they would tell me down at the precinct," he says. "It was surreal." Down at the precinct station "eventually, they fingerprinted me and booked me. I was booked on disturbing the peace and making a false report of a location of explosives. And when I was in my cell I found out they added a third charge about a hoax device." The police alleged that the stereo wires dangling from his fingers constituted a bomb threat.

"The Boston Police Department made a judgment that he was committing certain crimes and arrested him for disturbing the peace, making a false bomb threat, and possession of a hoax device," says David Procopio, press secretary for the Suffolk County district attorney's office. Previtera was held overnight. "The police woke me in the middle of the night and showed me pictures of U.S. soldiers with smiling Iraqi children," he says. "The officers told me these were pictures that I'd never see in the media, and that the *Boston Globe* and the *New York Times* were communist papers."

The next day the district attorney asked for $10,000 cash bail. But after the protesters showed the DA pictures of Previtera's protest, he reduced his request to $1,000. The judge had Previtera see a court psychiatrist, and then released him on his own recognizance. The *Boston Phoenix* and Boston Indymedia wrote stories about the arrest, drawing attention to the bogus charges.

On June 8, the district attorney's office essentially dropped the charges against Previtera. "We began a review of the facts to determine if any of the charges were warranted," says Procopio. "We spoke to police officers and witnesses, and after several days of our investigation, we determined that none of the charges were appropriate, and we basically terminated the prosecution."

"I was relieved," says Previtera. "But with torture continuing in U.S. military camps across the world, I'm keeping my good fortune in perspective."

IV

Watch Your Signs

1. A Passage from Revelations for Cheney—Renee Jensen

Renee Jensen of Elkins, West Virginia, likes to express herself. She has displayed a dozen signs in her yard, protesting the war in Iraq, Bush and Cheney, and the crackdown on civil liberties. Some of her signs have said:

> Mr. Bush, You're Fired.
> Mr. Ashcroft, We Prefer Our America Remain the Home of the Free and the Brave.
> Mr. Cheney, What You Sow You Shall Reap. Those Who Destroy the Earth Will Be Destroyed.
> Mr. Rumsfeld, Human Beings Are Not Just Collateral Damages, but People with Hopes, Dreams, Relationships, and Lives to Live.
> O, Evil Doers, Bush and Cheney Are Destroying America. I Cry Liberty and Stand for Our Constitution.
> Love One Another: War Is Dead Wrong.

In the fall of 2004 the Secret Service gave her a call.

"They said they wanted to ask me some questions," she recalls. "I said sure. They said someone called them and said I had signs up in my yard that were threatening the president. I said I did have some signs in my yard, but I wasn't threatening the president. The worst I've ever said was that he's an evildoer. And this Secret Service man specifically asked me about the sign about Mr. Cheney. He said, 'That's from Revelations.' I said, 'Yes, I have no desire to destroy anybody. I'm just quoting out of the Bible.' "

Then on January 11, 2005, the Secret Service paid her a visit. "I was actually taking a nap, and there was a knock on my door. There was a West Virginia state trooper and a Secret Service agent," she says, identifying them as Trooper R.J. Boggs and Agent James Lanham. "They asked to come in. And I let them. And they started interviewing me." Jensen, who at the time was running for city council, asked why they were there.

"Apparently someone had made a statement that I'd been canvassing door-to-door and had said I wanted to cut President Bush's head off," she says. "I told Agent Lanham that I was running for city council, but I hadn't started my door-to-door campaign yet, and I never had said anything like that." This didn't satisfy them, though. "They conducted an extensive interview about my background, my family, and any political organizations I belonged to. I told them I belong to the ACLU and that's about it."

They continued to pry, she says. Agent Lanham "asked me several times to sign a form about releasing my medical records, and I refused. That was kind of annoying. And he asked to search my house. He didn't have a search warrant, but I said go ahead. And they took some pictures of me and some pictures of my signs." Before they left, she says, "I had to sign a statement that I never threatened the president's life."

The Secret Service office in Charleston refused to give a comment to the *Charleston Gazette*, which broke the story, and my call to the Secret Service in Washington was not returned.

Jensen's problems didn't end with the Secret Service. The mayor of Elkins, Judy Guye, tried to use a city ordinance to make Jensen take her signs down. "Guye had said she believes Jensen's signs pose a potential traffic hazard, since people driving by her house often stop or slow down to look at them," Paul J. Nyden wrote in the *Charleston Gazette* on January 16, 2005. Nyden pointed out that the mayor, "a Republican, had a pro-Bush sign in her own front yard." Guye backed off.

Then one day Jensen's signs were vandalized. "I had gone to the movies, and when I came back, all my signs were stolen," Jensen says. "And one had been turned over, and someone wrote, 'We love George Bush' on it."

2. *"King George" Sign Attracts Secret Service—Derek Kjar*

It was August 26, 2004, and Derek Kjar, nineteen, was in the backyard of his home in Salt Lake City, stringing up plants in his garden. He got a voice mail message on his cell phone, so he decided to check it. "Derek, this is Agent Kim from the U.S. Secret Service, and I need to speak to you as soon as possible. Please call me," it said. Kim left his number, Kjar says. "At first, I thought it was a joke. My friend Marisa said, in jest, that they were trying to flag all the gay people in America." Kjar is gay. He called his mother for advice, and she told him to call the man back in the morning. That's what he did.

"Agent Kim answered," Kjar recalls. "He asked me where I was. I said I was at work. He said he'd be right there. I asked what it was about. And he said he couldn't disclose that over the phone." Kjar works at his family's dry-cleaning shop. He waited there until a silver Grand Am pulled up outside, and two agents came in, Agent Kim and another man.

"They said they had a call from my neighbor about a sticker on my car," he says. "And right then I knew exactly what they were talking about. It was a graphic I had printed off a Web site on my computer, and I just taped it onto my car with Scotch tape. It said: KING GEORGE—Off With His Head." The agents asked Kjar where the sticker was, so he took them out to his car. "I opened up the door and got it off the seat and handed it to them. They asked why it wasn't on the window anymore, and I said the sun had melted it off." That didn't satisfy them. "They started addressing me about how it could be a threat. They said it was 'borderline terrorism.' "

" 'Doesn't that take my freedom of speech away?' " Kjar recalls responding. No, the agents said, repeating the "borderline terrorism" charge. The agents then went inside with Kjar, and they interrogated him alone for another forty minutes. "They asked me if I was serious about making a threat to the president. And I said no, the only thing I was hoping to do was get a few people a little ticked off at me, or maybe get another vote for Kerry."

The questions continued. "They asked if I had ever made a threat to the president, or ever written to the president or contacted him in any way or ever met him," he says. "I said no, I had better things to do with my time. Then they asked me if I had ever studied assassination or terrorism, or the former assassination of other government officials, or ever read books in school about it, or done any school projects on it. I told them no, I hadn't. They asked if I had been in the military or any type of a militia groups. I was kind of baffled about that. 'No, no, no, not even close, way off.' "

To Kjar's relief, his mother finally arrived. "When my mother walked into the room, both agents stood up and puffed their chests out and said, 'You can't be in here,' " he recalls. "And my mother said, 'I don't give a shit. He's my son.' So she just sat right next to me and waited with me."

They proceeded to probe his political affiliations. "They asked me,

'Are you a part of an equal rights organization,' or blah, blah or any group opposed to the president?" They also got personal, he says. "They started asking me about my relationship with my roommates," he says. "And whether I went out to clubs. They asked whether I smoke, or drank, or took drugs. Then they started asking about my physical characteristics: If blond was my natural hair color, if I wore contacts, and if had any identifying marks, like tattoos, moles, and scars, and where they were or what they were from, and whether I had ever had any plastic surgery."

When they were done with the questioning the agents had an assignment for Kjar: "They asked me to write a statement about the sticker, why I got the sticker, where, how, and why I put it up." He complied.

Before they left they took three photographs of Kjar, and they warned him: "Do not post or print or hand out the sticker again." Kjar feels that his rights were violated, and that he was discriminated against. "I've almost lost my freedom of speech," he says. "I make one statement, and I get shot down, while everyone is out there with their bumper stickers and signs."

"The inference of a veiled threat is what we look at," says Special Agent Lon Garner of the Denver Secret Service office, who handles press calls in the West. "That's exactly what that was. By law, we investigate all those types of threats. We present those to the U.S. attorney. A veiled threat will always be investigated by the Secret Service. That's what we do. Always."

3. *Father of Soldier Told to Take Down "Impeach Bush"—Fred D'Amato*

Fred D'Amato was an early advocate of impeaching President Bush. D'Amato, who lives in Mount Pocono, Pennsylvania, wasn't shy about it. He put up a sign on his front lawn in early September 2003 that read: "Support Our Troops, Impeach Bush Admin."

It's personal for D'Amato. His son, Chris, was serving in Iraq at the time as part of the reserves. Morale was "not very good at all," Fred says, on the basis of Chris's e-mails home. What got Fred D'Amato boiling mad was when President Bush extended the term of duty for reservists in Iraq from one year to as much as eighteen months. "We tried calling up different politicians, but we got no answer from them, so I put up the sign." He displayed the sign, two feet wide by four feet high, in front of a large American flag.

According to the *Pocono Record*, one local resident of this city of three thousand complained to borough councilman Francis O'Boyle, who instructed the zoning officer to look into the matter. "The last couple of words is what's the problem," O'Boyle told the *Pocono Record*. "I don't think it's right to put a sign up like that and say those things. But it's up to the zoning officer."

Joseph W. Brady, zoning officer for the Mount Pocono borough, wrote a letter to Mr. and Mrs. D'Amato dated September 22, 2003, telling them that the sign violated a local ordinance. Wrote Brady:

> This sign must be removed immediately upon receipt of this letter, otherwise the Borough will be seeking Enforcement Remedies. . . . These penalties call for fines of up to $500 a day plus all court costs, including reasonable attorney fees. We ask your cooperation in removing this sign. If you wish to display a sign on your property, the necessary permits must be obtained. Of course this sign must meet all Borough Ordinances.

As soon as he opened the letter D'Amato called his wife at work. "She said to take it down immediately because we can't afford the $500 fine," he recalls. "I took it down for one day." He did not like the feeling of being gagged. "I felt angry and frustrated. It was definitely eliminating my free speech." Two neighbors he walks the dogs with in the mornings convinced him to put the sign back up. He also found three lawyers to work pro bono on his case and to put pressure on the city.

The Mount Pocono borough backed off, in part because of the bad publicity the story had generated. The *Pocono Record* wrote two critical editorials and a scathing column about the censorship, and the AP picked up the story. At a public meeting on October 6, 2003, Mount Pocono's lawyer, James Fareri, announced that the borough would suspend enforcement of the ordinance.

John Finnerty, borough council president, agreed but added: "All signs need a permit, for aesthetic reasons."

"You shouldn't need a permit to do something that's granted to you by the Constitution," D'Amato says.

4. Ticketed for "BUSHIT" Bumper Sticker—Denise Grier

Denise Grier is a nurse at Emory University Hospital in Georgia. On March 10, 2006, she was driving home from dinner when a DeKalb County police officer pulled her over. "I was just surprised because I hadn't done anything wrong," she says. "When he approached the car he had his hand on his weapon, and I was in my nurse's uniform with a stethoscope around my neck. He asked for my license, and then said, 'Any idea why I stopped you?'

"I said no.

" 'You have a lewd decal on your car.' "

Grier says she immediately thought that one of her kids had put something nasty on her bumper as a joke. "But then he mentioned the Bush sticker," she says. "That one says: 'I'm tired of all the BUSHIT.' "

(This story was first reported by Joe Johnson of the *Athens Banner-Herald*.) Grier says she told the officer it wasn't lewd, and that it was clearly a political statement. When he insisted it was lewd she said, "I'm not going to discuss this any further. Just give me the ticket." Which he did. Under "offense," it said: "Lewd decals."

The ticket was for $100.

She didn't pay it. "It's not just a Democrat/Republican issue," she says. "Y'all need to get beyond that. It's my right to speak, and yours." Gerry Weber, the legal director of the ACLU of Georgia, represents Grier. "The indicators are that the officer didn't like her views of President Bush, and that was the motivating factor," he says. He says the ticketing was clearly illegal. The Georgia Supreme Court had struck down the "lewd bumper sticker" statute way back in 1991, in a case involving a defendant who had a "Shit Happens" bumper sticker. This shouldn't keep happening fifteen years later, he says.

The DeKalb County Police Department would not discuss the facts of the case. "We don't comment on other officers' tickets," says officer Herschel Grangent, who handles media affairs. "That officer is making his decision on the street."

On April 4, 2006, Judge R. Joy Walker dismissed the case. Grier was not surprised. "I knew it was going to happen," she says. "It was pretty much a no-brainer."

By the way, this is not the first time someone in Grier's family has gotten into trouble over a bumper sticker. In 2005, she says, her twenty-year-old son was pulled over in Athens, Georgia, for having a bumper sticker that said:

Bush sucks
Dick
Cheney too.

She says the police officer told her son, "If you do not remove the bumper sticker, I'm taking you to jail." So he removed it. "He thought it was kind of funny," though she told her son she would rather go to jail than take her bumper sticker off. In October 2006 Grier filed suit against the county police department. She alleges that she was deprived of her First Amendment, Fourth Amendment, and Fourteenth Amendment rights.

"It was outrageous," Grier said in a statement. "He pulled me over for his own political agenda, and grossly abused his authority in violating my free speech."

She tells me, "I decided to sue because unfortunately in the United States it's the only way you can get something done. Until you do something punitive, nothing changes."

V

Happy Holidays

1. Peace Postponed on July 4—Brainerd, Minnesota

Brainerd, Minnesota, is a town of 56,000 people, and like most towns it has a Fourth of July parade. In 2003, the Brainerd Area Coalition for Peace (BACP) requested to march in the parade. But Brainerd Community Action, the group sponsoring the parade, turned down the coalition's request after consulting with Brainerd city attorney Tom Fitzpatrick. The parade organizers said they were worried about the safety of the protesters.

"Your decision to deny our participation in the 2003 Brainerd 4th of July Celebration Parade is in violation of our rights, illegal, discriminatory, and arbitrary," wrote Larry Fisk, a member of the peace coalition, to Fitzpatrick and Nancy L. Cross, the executive director of Brainerd Community Action, on July 2. The decision, added Fisk, "makes a mockery of what the day and the celebration are supposed to be about: FREEDOM! The freedom of Americans in all our diversity of creed, color, and opinion." Fisk urged them to change their minds.

Fitzpatrick and Cross declined.

Afterward, Fisk wrote a commentary in the *Brainerd Daily Dispatch* that said in part:

BACP would like to be educating the public about the unnecessary and terrible human toll of the latest war and advocating peace rather than defending our right to speak. But this is one of our basic civil liberties and should be of concern to all citizens. If BACP can be barred, who else? . . . Do we have freedoms in America, or do we just pretend?

Kristen Blann, another member of the peace group, picks up on Fisk's argument: "At the parade there were religious groups handing out leaflets that said, 'Are you good enough to go to heaven?' There was a range of views being expressed, so why weren't ours allowed? Why would we, of all of the groups, be a threat to public safety? It seems like a cover for protecting people from hearing a message they don't want to hear."

Sara Dunlap, who has lived in Brainerd for thirty-four years, is also a member of the peace group. "We were shocked when they refused us," she says. "The parade's always been open. When we applied to march they said there were openings. 'Oh, yeah, just send it in,' they said. But then they said it was a safety issue. They didn't want us to get hurt, oh bless their hearts."

Dunlap says the peace coalition had planned on being nonconfrontational. "We were going to be low-key. We were going to carry a peace flag and an American flag and be respectful. We weren't going to say anything about oil or badmouth Bush. We were going to carry 'Veterans for Peace' signs that said 'We Support the Troops: Bring Them Home.' " Being denied the right to march was like "a personal slap in the face," she says. "I've poured my guts out for this town. I was on the board of directors of Community Action in the seventies. I've been on practically every board in this town. And after all the time I put in for this community it disappointed me so much that they could say I couldn't march. I'm very disgusted."

The peace coalition contacted the American Civil Liberties Union of Minnesota (ACLU-MN). "You can't make this stuff up," says Chuck Samuelson, executive director.

The peace group and ACLU-MN threatened to sue the city of Brainerd and Community Action. On March 22, 2004, the parties reached a settlement.

Though the city and Community Action asserted in a statement that was part of the agreement that their actions "were motivated by good faith concerns about public safety and did not reflect any intent to deprive BACP or its members of their constitutional rights," they also recognized the need to "accommodate the First Amendment rights of diverse community participants." They admitted that "BACP was unable to exercise its free speech rights in the 2003 Fourth of July parade." And they agreed to establish procedures that "must be neutral with respect to the content of the speech or message of any proposed parade participant."

The peace group eschewed a monetary award. Instead, as part of the settlement, it got the city to agree to put on a symposium, "The Right to Free Speech in the 21st Century Under the United States and Minnesota Constitutions." The city and Community Action also said they would "welcome participation by the BACP in the 2004 Fourth of July parade." The peace group did participate, with 125 people joining, making it the largest contingent in the parade.

Protesters held signs that said "Peace Is Patriotic," and they had a float with two coffins on it, according to the *Brainerd Daily Dispatch*. One, with an American flag on it, had a sign that read "Over 800 American Dead." The other, with an Iraqi flag, said: "10,000 Civilian Dead."

2. Antiwar Vets Booted from Vets Day—Tallahassee, Florida

On Veterans Day 2003 in Tallahassee, a group of thirty vets were not allowed to march in the Veterans Day parade. The reason: They opposed Bush's Iraq War.

"Members of Veterans for Peace and Vietnam Veterans Against the War were yanked off a downtown Tallahassee street, directly in front of the Old Capitol, while marching in the holiday parade they had legitimately registered in," wrote J. Taylor Rushing of the *Florida Times-Union*. Others were allowed to keep marching, including the usual high school marching bands and—get this—"even a group of young women from the local Hooters restaurant."

The antiwar vets were passing out leaflets and holding banners that said "Honor the Warrior, Not the War" and "Support the Troops, Bring Them Home." "We'd gone in and filled out a little form and paid our ten bucks to get into the parade and everything, but when we showed up the parade marshals said we couldn't be in it," Tom Baxter of Veterans for Peace tells me. Baxter tried to disregard the marshal. "I said, 'I'm not paying any attention to you. You've got to get a cop over here.' So a policeman came over and said, 'You can't be in the parade. It's their parade.' I was pissed," he recalls.

The VFW had sponsored the parade, and while Baxter, a Vietnam vet, is a member of that organization too, he was still denied entry.

"They can have their free speech, just not in the parade. They belong on the sidewalk," parade chair Ken Conroy told the *Florida Times-Union*. The newspaper itself agreed with that position. Its November 14, 2003, editorial, "Free Speech: Wrong Time and Place," said,

> The parade sponsored by the Veterans of Foreign Wars was intended solely to honor those who had served their country. It was

not a forum on political issues. Yet, a few marchers tried to use it to publicize their opposition to the liberation of Iraq. . . . Let protesters protest on their own time, with their own parade.

Baxter wrote a letter to the editor, taking the paper to task for its position. He said that the parade actually was a forum for political issues. "Political candidates and officials were in the parade passing out campaign literature. That this was a private function is open to question." Several other people also told the paper that the antiwar vets should have been allowed to march.

But others were hostile. R.J. Collins, a Vietnam vet, wrote a letter to the *Tallahassee Democrat*, denouncing the protesters' "negative political agenda [that] would demean the day."

And he went further.

American protests against the war serve the enemy by strengthening his cause and fueling his will to aggressively attack our troops. These protests also lower our troops' morale and concentration. . . . Your protests have helped to kill our soldiers just as sure as the enemy.

Baxter said his group considered suing. But the outcry about the group's exclusion was enough to convince the VFW not to sponsor the parade in 2004 and 2005. Instead, Leon County took it over.

"We've been in the parade ever since," says Baxter.

3. *On Memorial Day, Peace Banners Too Bold—Boulder, Colorado*

Every Memorial Day in Boulder, Colorado, for more than twenty-five years a 10K race has ended up at the University of Colorado's Folsom

Stadium. The event also comes with military trimmings. On May 30, 2005, some soldiers wore their colors, there was a twenty-one-gun salute, and air force jets flew over in formation. A private group called Bolder Boulder sponsors the race, one of the largest in the country, with the 2005 event drawing 47,000 participants.

Some peace activists wanted to participate in a different way, by expressing their views in the stadium. In 2004 and 2005, they were not permitted to do so. A few days before the 2005 event Bolder Boulder told members of the Rocky Mountain Peace and Justice Center that they would not be able to display their banners in the stadium. "They will not permit us to banner or use the Folsom field and other facilities, claiming that these state-owned facilities at the University of Colorado are not a public forum," the peace group said in a statement on its Web site. "But we, as taxpayers of Colorado, own that facility and heartily disagree, finding that nothing in state law or university rules allows them to place such restrictions on us. Fundamental federal law, our Constitution, and its Bill of Rights, support us."

To test that claim, and to express their opposition to the Iraq War, three members of the group went to Folsom Stadium on the morning of Memorial Day 2005. Carolyn Bninski, fifty-five, Joanne Cowan, fifty-five, and Ellen Stark, fifty-eight, entered at the gate, climbed the stadium stairs, and stood at the back so they weren't blocking anyone's view. They then unfurled the banner "End the Occupation of Iraq Now."

"The security people came running up and said, 'Take that banner down,'" says Stark. After she and her two colleagues refused to budge, "the security officers began twisting the banner out of our arms, and one of the guys squeezed my neck with a couple of his fingers."

That made her let go of the banner.

They then looked through the backpacks of the women to see if they had any other banners. "They said if we put up another banner we would be arrested," she says. The women didn't have any more banners, but friends of the activists had carried one in for them: "Protect Free Speech." "We got that banner, and we held that up," says Stark. "Then they were really mad, and they escorted us outside."

She says the police did not want to arrest them or give them a citation, but the protesters were intent on challenging the policy in court. "We said it was very important to see what the law was" on free speech. "I finally said that maybe we'll just go back in and put up another banner, which another friend had brought in. This one said 'No Blood for Oil.' Once they heard that, they decided to ticket us." The women were charged with "improper conduct on public property."

Lieutenant Tim McGraw, a thirty-two-year veteran of the University of Colorado police force, says the event was private. What's more, university policy prohibits such displays. "In various buildings and facilities, including the stadium, there are various rules and regulations—one cannot smoke or have alcohol, for instance. There's also a rule that one cannot hold up banners, because it blocks people's views." McGraw believes the protest was a publicity stunt. "It became very obvious that they were seeking media attention. They wanted to gain notoriety."

Cliff Bosley, the race director and son of the founder of the event, agrees. "They were more interested in garnering press as opposed to what their real message was," he says. "We met with them three days before the race, and said, 'Look, here's the deal: It doesn't really matter what the cause is, if we let one cause in, we've got to let them all in.' And Boulder is a town of causes. And some want to stand on the Bolder Boulder shoulders. Our stance was, we are not going to open the door to people who want to make a statement about prairie dogs, so we said no, with the caveat that we can still create a place for you guys to be. We gave them three or four different ideas—locations along the road race—but they didn't want to do that."

Judd Golden, who is chair of the Boulder County ACLU, worked with the three women in his capacity as a private attorney. He says their tickets were "totally inappropriate." He has a problem "when you tear down banners and eject people and say you can't display this message, and if you do, we'll charge you with a crime." The charges against the women ultimately were dropped, but they were unable to hold their banners in the stadium at the 2006 Bolder Boulder event.

4. Peace Activists Get Death Threats, Police Stand By— Rochester, Minnesota

On March 30, 2003, in Rochester, Minnesota, prowar organizers put together a Support the Troops rally, which three thousand people attended at a public park called Soldiers Memorial Field. About thirty members of the Southeastern Minnesota Alliance of Peacemakers decided to attend in silent protest. "Support the Troops: Bring Them Home" was one of their signs. Shortly after the peacemakers entered the park the police asked them to leave, says Steve Schwen, an organic farmer, who was vice chair of the alliance.

"We said, 'We're here to support the troops,'" Schwen recalled.

"You're not invited," they said.

"Well, this is a public park," he said.

"This park is rented for the day, by invitation only," the police responded.

Barb Fix, founder of Rural Peacemakers, was also at Soldiers Memorial Field to protest the war. She says she had heard commercials on TV and radio that invited everyone to attend. "We considered ourselves invited," she says.

The police didn't buy it. "They said, 'Get out of here, or you will be arrested.' They told us to go across the street," Schwen says. And about ten police officers pushed the peace protesters back. Members of the Support the War crowd heaped abuse on the peace activists. "They were calling us traitors and saying we should be tried for treason, and telling us to go to Cuba, China, or France," recalls Fix.

Then things really turned ugly. "Three individuals threatened to get their guns and kill us," says Schwen. Fix remembers one of them saying, "I'm going to go home and get my gun." Schwen says they were making these threats within earshot of the police, who were only about ten feet away. "I turned to a police officer and said, 'This man is threatening to kill me.' And the police officer said, 'I didn't hear it. Did you get it on tape?' And did nothing." Despite Schwen's pleas the police did not apprehend the individuals or even take down their names.

"I don't have any information about threats being made with officers present," said Captain Jim Pittenger, head of investigations for the Rochester Police Department.

No one was ever charged in the incident.

"I've really not been that visible and vocal since," says Schwen. "It's a little bit intimidating. I have a family."

VI

Welcome to Our Place of Business

1. Denny's Manager: "We Don't Serve bin Ladens Here"

Max Morgan is not his given name. That would be Ehab Mohamed.

In August 2003, the Egyptian American insurance broker who lives in Florida decided to change it. Though he says he had experienced no harassment up to that point, he didn't want to take any chances. "I did it just to avoid unpleasant incidents, having heard on TV and read in the papers about some ugly incidents that had happened."

Five months later Morgan was unable to avoid an unpleasant incident. He and six friends, all with Middle Eastern backgrounds, headed off on a fishing trip to Islamorada in the Florida Keys. As they were driving down they decided to stop at a Denny's restaurant in Florida City, at about two in the morning on January 11, 2004.

"We were all exhausted and hungry," Morgan recalls. "We walked in, we were seated, there was nothing unusual. The waitress was really friendly, and she took our drink order." Then they ordered food: veggie omelettes and oatmeal, Morgan says. The food never arrived.

They waited for about an hour. Other customers who had come in after them had gotten their meals already. One of Morgan's friends, Ehab AlBaradi, had been wondering for quite a while what was taking so long. But his buddies told him just to wait. Finally, AlBaradi got up to ask what was going on. He approached the shift manager, Eduardo Ascano. "AlBaradi asked Ascano if he was the restaurant's manager, and Ascano replied: 'Bin Laden is the manager,' " according to the $28 million lawsuit that Morgan, AlBaradi, and the five others have filed against Ascano and the franchise owner.

AlBaradi asked again, and Ascano allegedly repeated: "Bin Laden is in charge." AlBaradi then asked whether there was a problem in the kitchen. "You don't get it," Ascano allegedly responded. "Bin Laden is in charge in the kitchen, too!" When AlBaradi returned to his table "he was quiet, and his face was rather yellow," Morgan says. When AlBaradi told them what had happened they decided to leave.

On their way out one of the men, Usama El-A-Baidy, asked Ascano if he had said "bin Laden" to AlBaradi. Ascano confirmed it, according to the lawsuit, and added the following: "I say whatever the fuck I want to say! . . . We don't serve bin Ladens here! . . . You guys, out! You're not to come here anymore." As it happens, two police officers were eating at that Denny's at the time. Officer Estrellita Dion Brutto of the Miami-Dade Police Department took the side of the manager.

"She was really off the wall," says Morgan. "We tried to explain to her what happened, and we asked her to file a police report on the incident." Instead, she ordered them out of the restaurant. "We asked her for her name and badge number. And she refused to give it to us. She said, 'If you want my name and badge number, you're going to have to get it on your arrest records.' " At that point, she pulled out her handcuffs. Morgan and his party paid for their drinks and left.

"That was a really scary moment," he says, "because you know your rights, and you know the law protects you, and you know you didn't do anything wrong, and it's her job to protect us and our civil rights, and yet she insisted on participating in the wrongdoing." Brutto declined to comment. "Officer Brutto will not be conducting any interviews regarding this matter," says Detective Alvaro Zabaleta in the media relations bureau of the Miami-Dade Police Department.

But Brutto told the Florida Commission on Human Relations that she had not heard the manager make derogatory comments; that one or two of the men went behind the counter to yell at the cook; and that the most aggressive one smelled of alcohol. She also said that one of the men grabbed the manager's tie and threatened to beat him up, but the commission found that hard to believe. "This occurrence is highly unlikely," it noted, since no one else saw it and the manager himself denied it. The waitress, Germaine Henry, told the commission that the customers were polite and sober, and she confirmed that her manager had made comments about bin Laden.

Suffice it to say that once they got in their car, Morgan and his friends—AlBaradi, El-A-Baidy, Nabil Arafat, Esam Hessein, Mohammad Natour, and Usama Mohamed—were rattled. "We were in a state of shock," Morgan says. By the time they reached Islamorada no one was in the mood for fishing. In fact, they never fished the whole weekend. "Your desires are not the same. Your mind is preoccupied. You're really confused about your identity, your sense of belonging."

Morgan, who is a permanent resident, says he owns and operates insurance companies in seven states and has four thousand clients. "This is my home," he says. "This is where my friends are. This is where my business is. My future plans are here. If you're rejected it's really hard to live with. How can you go to work the next day with a positive attitude with this thought in the back of your mind, that everyone thinks you're worthless or inferior and should be treated with no dignity and no respect?"

He decided to contact his attorney, Alan Kauffman of Becker & Po-
liakoff. Kauffman filed a complaint on behalf of Morgan and his friends
with the Florida Commission on Human Relations, which ruled in
their favor in January 2005. "There is reasonable cause to believe that
an unlawful employment practice occurred," it concluded. In the
spring of 2005 Kauffman and his clients filed suit against the fran-
chisee, Restaurant Collection, Inc., for "unlawful race, religious, and
national origin discrimination" and for "negligent retention/supervi-
sion." And they sued Ascano for "intentional infliction of emotional
distress." Alfonso Fernandez owns Restaurant Collection, Inc. "We
are truly committed to treating all of our guests with respect, and we
take every guest concern seriously," he wrote in a statement after the
suit was filed. "These allegations of discrimination were immediately
and thoroughly investigated by an independent, outside agency that
found no evidence whatsoever to support the guests' claims." Reached
for comment in June 2006, Fernandez said: "I really am not prepared
to talk to you about this situation." Fernandez's lawyer, C. Richard
Fulmer, gave me a one-sentence response to the claims in the lawsuit:
"We deny the allegations."

Ascano's lawyer, Eduardo Cosio, would not return multiple
phone calls, and I could not locate a number for Ascano. When he
talked to the Florida Commission on Human Relations "Mr. Ascano
denied making any derogatory comments about the customers or
their ethnicity," it noted. "Mr. Ascano stated that the Complainant and
his companions came into the restaurant drunk and were loud and
disorderly."

Denny's, which is not a party to the lawsuit, issued a statement on
April 29, 2005. "The allegations have been found to be baseless," said
Nelson J. Marchioli, CEO and president of Denny's. "We intend to aggressively challenge the accusations. We are confident when all of the
facts are presented that Denny's will be vindicated." Morgan believes

that the restaurant misjudged the determination of the plaintiffs. "They thought we would not pursue this because of the general public opinion about us," he says. "They thought that we'd just give in, and hide and swallow it, and not do anything about it, but we decided otherwise."

The case is still pending.

2. Santorum Aide, State Trooper Toss Young Women Out of Barnes & Noble

On the evening of August 10, 2005, Hannah Shaffer of Glen Mills, Pennsylvania, decided to go to the nearby Barnes & Noble outside of Wilmington, Delaware. She wanted to see then Pennsylvania senator Rick Santorum, who was promoting his book *It Takes a Family*. The event was billed as a "book signing and discussion," Shaffer says.

Shaffer, eighteen, thought Santorum's public appearance might be a good occasion to have a discussion with him about his claim that legalizing gay marriage was akin to legalizing incest and bestiality. "So I contacted a few of my left-leaning friends, and they said they'd really like to be there because they felt the same way," she says. When she arrived early, at 6:00 P.M., some of her friends were already there, along with two other young women she didn't know, Stacey Galperin and Miriam Rocek.

As Shaffer was talking with her friends Rocek made a joke.

She held up a copy of a book by the gay writer Dan Savage called *The Kid*, which is about how he and his partner adopted a son. And Rocek said, "It would be funny if we got Santorum to sign this book." (To discredit Santorum, Savage and his readers in 2003 came up with a nasty definition of "Santorum" that now often appears on Internet searches for Santorum's name.) A woman nearby was not amused. "You're shameful and disgusting," she said, according to Shaffer.

A state trooper in full official uniform, including hat and gun, was in the store, and, according to Shaffer and Galperin, he met with the woman and a few others, including one of Santorum's people. Galperin says she heard the trooper ask, "Do you want me to get rid of them?" And then the trooper, Delaware State Police sergeant Mark DiJiacomo, who was on detail as a private security guard, came over to the group of women.

Here is the conversation, as Galperin remembers it:

"You guys have to leave."

"Why?"

"Your business is not wanted here. They don't want you here anymore. If you don't leave, you're going to be arrested. If you can't post bail you'll go to prison. Those of you who are under eighteen will go to Ferris [the juvenile detention center]. And those of you over eighteen will go either to Gander Hill Prison or the woman's correctional facility. Any questions?"

Shaffer decided to leave with her friends.

Galperin and Rocek decided to stay.

"That's it," he told them, according to Galperin. "You're under arrest. Give me your ID. You're going to prison." Sergeant DiJiacomo allegedly led the two out to his police car. "You're going to embarrass your families," he told them, she recalls. "Your names are going to be all over the paper." And he told them they wouldn't be able to get into college. He told Rocek to put her hands on the squad car, and then told both of them to call their parents and tell them to bring "at least $1,000 in bail money," Galperin says.

Galperin reached her father, an attorney. "I told my dad, 'I'm under arrest for expressing dissenting opinions.'" Her father asked to speak to the sergeant.

"Your dad says get out of here," the sergeant told her. "He'll meet you at home." And he banned them from the store and the mall. And so they both left.

By this time Hannah Shaffer had managed to reach her mother, Heidi, on the phone, who was planning on going to the event anyway. "She came and said, whoever wants to return to the bookstore should come with her, and we would talk respectfully to the police officer and to Barnes & Noble about why they had kicked us out and threatened to arrest us," Shaffer says. Six or seven of the kids went back to the parking lot at Barnes & Noble with Heidi. "We were standing outside in the parking lot, and my mother went into the store to find out what happened," Shaffer says. "Just as she entered the officer came out, and he saw us, and he drove over in his car very fast."

He was not happy. "You're under arrest. Get into the car," he said.

"But my mom took us over here and wanted to speak to you."

"Do I look like your mother? You're not wanted here. You had your chance. You showed up again. Now you're under arrest." Instead of arresting them, though, he threatened them once more and told them never to go to the bookstore or the mall again. At that point he let Shaffer and the other young women leave.

"I was pretty upset," she says.

So was her mother when she came out of the store and heard what had happened. "I actually tried to talk humanely to the policeman," she says. "He told me, if I took any of the underaged kids in, I would be charged with contributing to the delinquency of a minor."

Heidi Shaffer says she is most upset about the strong-arm tactics of DiJiacomo. "One of the girls came home and was hysterical for about two days," she says. "Some even were afraid to tell their parents. That this hired gun can say whatever he wants and terrorize these kids is very, very scary. This is unconscionable." DiJiacomo did not return my phone calls seeking comment.

"From all indications that we have, he handled his duties and responsibilities appropriately," said Lieutenant Joseph Aviola, director of public affairs for the Delaware State Police, at the time. Aviola says two customers warned DiJiacomo that the young women were planning a disturbance, and that there had been a previous incident at a book signing with Santorum.

At Barnes & Noble's headquarters Mary Ellen Keating, senior vice president for corporate communications and public affairs, denies that the store had anything to do with it. "I spoke to the assistant manager, and what she told me was that the store management was not consulted on how the situation was managed," she says. "A state policeman, without consulting management, removed these students from the store."

On May 30, 2006, Galperin, Rocek, Hannah Shaffer, and Heidi Shaffer, along with one minor, sued DiJiacomo. They also sued an unidentified "member of Senator Santorum's promotional team." They are seeking "redress for the deprivation of their First and Fourth Amendment rights and for the emotional distress caused by DiJiacomo's false arrest and unlawful threats," the lawsuit says. Ralph Durstein, deputy attorney general for the State of Delaware, is representing DiJiacomo. "Mark DiJiacomo more or less tried to serve as an intermediary between the campaign folks and the manager of the Barnes & Noble on the one side and some pretty unhappy folks on the other," Durstein says. Santorum's spokesperson, Virginia Davis, would not comment about the suit.

Barnes & Noble had nothing to do with the alleged violation of rights, says the lawsuit, brought by the Delaware and Pennsylvania affiliates of the ACLU. "No Barnes & Noble employee or agent ever instructed Defendant DiJiacomo to have Plaintiffs ejected," the lawsuit says. "No Barnes & Noble employee or agent ever instructed Plaintiffs to leave the store." The plaintiffs are seeking an admission that their rights were violated, attorneys' fees, and "nominal, compensatory, and punitive damages in an amount to be proven at trial."

3. Muslim American Reporter Questioned at Black & Decker— Ayesha Ahmad

It was midday on November 22, 2002, and Ayesha Ahmad was on assignment in Easton, Maryland. A reporter for Capital News Service out of the University of Maryland, she was covering the closing of the Black & Decker plant there, the largest employer in the area. Ahmad, a North Carolina native, was wearing her hijab, a traditional Muslim scarf, as she approached the gate of the plant.

"I asked the guard what the deal was with media, and he said the plant did not want media on the property, but there was no problem if I wanted to talk to employees off the property," Ahmad recalls. "So I just stood across the street from the entrance of the plant." At first she had no luck getting people's attention. "The only way I could think to stop them was to stand there with a sign, so I wrote up on a piece of notebook paper: 'Black & Decker Employees—Willing to Talk to a Reporter?' People would slow down to read the sign, but nobody stopped." Except a couple of police officers.

"I walked toward them and said, 'Am I not supposed to be here?' "

"No, no, it's fine you're here," they told her, according to Ahmad. "But someone called you in as a suspicious-looking person of Middle Eastern descent." Ahmad didn't take it seriously. "I started laughing," she says. "They asked me what I was doing. I told them I was a reporter. And they didn't even ask to see my card," adding that the police treated her respectfully and then left her alone. She assumes that whoever called the police "was just some stupid person who was ignorant and didn't know what else to do," and says that she has information that the call came from one of the buildings across from the plant.

But the police say Black & Decker actually made the call. Black & Decker had no comment. "We received a call from Black & Decker personnel of a suspicious person," says Easton police chief George Harvey. "The issue of Muslim garb—I don't think it had an effect. I think it was more of an unauthorized person on the premises, but I'm not saying it had no effect."

4. Lawyer Nabbed in Mall for Wearing Peace T-Shirt He Bought There— Stephen F. Downs

Stephen F. Downs was not the political type. But then some activists in his church told him they were kicked out of Crossgates Mall in December 2002 near Albany, New York, just for wearing antiwar T-shirts. One simply said "Peace on Earth."

"As a lawyer, I was very offended" that they were kicked out, says Downs, who was the head lawyer for New York's Commission on Judicial Conduct at that time. Downs also was troubled by George W. Bush's lead-up to the Iraq War. "I felt there was absolutely no justification for the war," he says. "It seemed illegal, irrational. And I had a gut feeling they were lying."

So on March 3, 2003, he decided to express himself.

"I wanted to say something, that I was opposed to this war that was impending," he explains. "It happened that there was a store in the mall that did T-shirts. I mentioned it to my son, Roger, who was thirty-one at the time, and he said, 'Yeah, I feel the same way. Mind if I come with?' So we went down there after work, and we went into the T-shirt shop." Downs chose to have "Peace on Earth" on one side and

"Give Peace a Chance" on the other. His son chose "No War with Iraq" and "Let Inspections Work."

Rather than leave the shirts in a bag, they put them on right away and headed to the food court. "On our way," says Downs, "I saw a teenager who said, 'I love that T-shirt,' and asked me, 'Where can I get one?' So I took them back and introduced them to the owner of the T-shirt shop."

After Downs and his son got to the food court and ordered something to eat, "security people started circling around," he recalls. "We went up and said, 'What's up?' And they said, 'We want you to take off those T-shirts.' And I said, 'No, I don't want to do that.' " The security guards then told them to leave the mall. "I said I didn't want to do that, either." So Downs and his son sat back down.

Soon a police officer joined the guards. "Look, you're going to have to take off these T-shirts or leave the mall," he told Downs. "And I said I wasn't going to do that. So he said, 'I'll have to arrest you.' Finally, I said, 'Look, you do what you need to do, I'm not going to take my T-shirt off,' and I held out my hands, and he put handcuffs on me." Roger, not wanting to get arrested, took his shirt off.

The police took Downs to a station that was in the mall, and then to the courthouse to be arraigned on trespassing charges. He was let out on his own recognizance. As soon as the media picked up the story "all hell broke loose," Downs remembers. He was getting phone calls from as far away as Australia and Turkey, he says.

Two days after his arrest an activist group, Women Against War, organized a protest at the mall. "About a hundred people showed up wearing political T-shirts," he says. This time the mall did nothing. "They were realizing they had a public relations disaster on their hands," Downs says.

Two weeks later, at his court date, no witnesses from the mall appeared to testify against him, so the DA was forced to drop the charges. One year later Downs and the New York Civil Liberties Union sued the local police and the mall owner, Pyramid Management Group. The case is pending.

"What we're trying to establish is that people don't give up their liberties when they enter a mall," says Downs.

VII

Trouble on the Job

1. Graphic Designer Loses Job After Heckling Bush—Glenn Hiller

Glenn Hiller is a graphic designer, and he wanted to convey a message to President Bush. The president was scheduled to speak on August 17, 2004, at Hedgesville High School, which is near Hiller's home in Berkeley Springs, West Virginia. He says he asked his boss at the design firm where he worked whether he could take part of that afternoon off to go hear Bush and to try to ask him a question or two.

"I got a ticket through a woman we do work with in the advertising community," he says. "She and my boss both had full knowledge of my political position, and they had knowledge that I was going to ask a question when I was there." They knew, he says, that "I'm not a fan of Bush." Hiller says his boss let him off early so he could go.

"I got there just in time to hear him speak," Hiller recalls. "And while I was listening to the speech, I didn't know if I was going to have the nerve to speak up. But then he started to talk about 9/11, and immediately rolled that into the war on Iraq, as though one had anything to do with the other. That aggravated me. And then he was defending his reasons for going to war, saying Saddam Hussein may not have had weapons of mass destruction, but he did have the capability to make them. At that point, I shouted out, 'That's not the same thing!' "

As Bush continued to talk about the war, Hiller piped up again: "Would you be willing to sacrifice your children for the liberation of Iraq?" And when Bush moved on to boast about the economy Hiller interrupted one final time. "I asked, 'Explain how the outsourcing of American jobs is good for the American economy.' " Hiller believes he reached the president's ear. "I know he heard me," says Hiller, "because he quipped at one point, 'Isn't it great that we live in a free country where people are free to voice their opinions?' And it was roughly then that I was escorted out by two campaign officials, who threatened to have me arrested." Hiller says he defended his right to free speech. "I told the campaign workers I had every right to be here," he says. "I told them, I'm a citizen of this community. And I'm not doing anything wrong. I have a right and an obligation to get involved."

The Bush people told him he was being disruptive, he says, and that "this isn't the time or place." But Hiller disagreed. "My argument was that there is no venue, there is no place for a regular person, particularly one who disagrees with the president, to ask him a genuine question. He only makes appearances at completely scripted events, and only surrounds himself with people who completely agree with him."

Hiller paid an immediate price for his outspokenness. "I showed up for work the next day, and my boss told me my actions were unacceptable and reflected bad on the company, and she said she had to let me go," he recalls. "I said, 'What do you mean?'"

"She said, basically, a client was offended, and she couldn't have that."

2. Boss Boots Employee for Kerry Bumper Sticker—Lynne Gobbell

Lynne Gobbell ran the bagging machine at Enviromate, in Moulton, Alabama, for about two years. On September 9, 2004, she was fired, she says, because her boss, Phil Geddes, demanded that she take a Kerry/Edwards bumper sticker off her car, and she refused to do so. (Geddes did not return a phone call or e-mail for comment.) The story of Gobbell's firing first appeared in the *Decatur Daily*. It reported her account that Geddes had put a flyer in employees' envelopes that lauded the Bush tax cut. Here's what the flyer said, according to the paper.

> Just so you will know, because of the Bush tax (cut):
> I was able to buy the new Hammer Mill.
> I was able to finance our receivables.
> I was able to get the new CAT skid steer.
> I was able to get the wire cutter.
> I was able to give you a job. . . .
> You got the benefit of the Bush tax cut. Everyone did.

Gobbell tells me how she realized she was in trouble. "The first time I found out something was wrong was right after first break, when we were going back to work. The plant production manager told me, 'Phil says take that sticker off your car, or you're fired.' "

"I told him, 'Phil can't tell me who to vote for.' " The plant manager, Dennis Cantrell, told Gobbell to go tell him that herself, she says. "So I go in there and I said, 'Phil, did you tell me to take that sticker off my car?'

"He said, 'I sure did.'

"I told him, 'You can't tell me who to vote for.'

"He said, 'I own this place.'

"And then I told him he still couldn't tell me who to vote for. And he told me to get out.

"And I asked him, 'Am I fired?'"

"And he said, 'I'm thinking about it.'"

"And I asked him again, and he hollered, 'Get out, and shut the door.' "

Gobbell says she asked plant manager Cantrell whether she should leave or go back to work. And he told her to go back to work. "I hadn't been there a minute when Cantrell came back and said, 'I reckon you're fired.' Phil told him to tell me that I could either work for him or John Kerry." How did she react? "I took my gloves off and threw them in the garbage can, and took my purse and left. I really couldn't believe it."

A few days later the phone rang, and it was Senator Kerry on the line. "He was telling me how proud of me he was for standing up to my boss, and how he had read what my boss had said," she says. "And Senator Kerry told me, 'Have him know from today that you're working for me. You're hired.' "

3. Red Cross Gets Blue in the Face—H. Thayer Kingsbury

You can volunteer for the Red Cross for fifty years, but if you have peace signs on your car, you're not welcome in its lot. That's what H. Thayer Kingsbury of Keene, New Hampshire, found out.

Kingsbury had volunteered for the New Hampshire West chapter of the American Red Cross for more than five decades. A pillar of his community, he had done his share of public service. He had served "a stint as county chairman," according to the *Keene Sentinel*, which broke this story. He also was a state representative for eight years. But his good work got him nowhere.

On March 25, 2003, he was volunteering as usual at the Red Cross, and he parked his car in the parking lot. "I had stickers on my car: 'We support our troops but not the Mad George war' and 'Support our troops, not the war. Impeach Bush,' " he tells me. A Red Cross staffer told Kingsbury that "either the signs had to go, or the car had to go," the *Sentinel* reported. Kingsbury removed the signs, "but the more he thought about it, the more outraged he became that he wasn't being allowed to express his opinion," the paper noted.

So he wrote a letter of resignation, in which he said: "I cannot give my time or monetary support to an organization that abrogates my constitutional right to free speech and expression." Andrea Johnson, who was the executive director of the New Hampshire West chapter of the American Red Cross at the time, says she wasn't there that day, but that she "absolutely" believes that her staff did the right thing. "Thayer's vehicle was parked right in front of our entrance," she tells me. "He had big signs, and they weren't just antiwar but anti-Bush, and it was offensive to some of the people coming into our building." She says those signs violate the Red Cross's principles of "neutrality and impartiality."

Leaders of the local Red Cross chapter urged Kingsbury to reconsider. But rejoining the Red Cross is "not in the cards," he says. "The idea that a local organization would make this a requirement is by itself amazing." It is indicative of "what is happening as far as our constitutional rights go. I'm eighty-two. I'm concerned about what is going to happen to my children and grandchildren. I thought I'd at least stand up for my concern."

4. Borders Pulls Plug on Musician Who Joked About Bush's Legs— *Julia Rose*

Julia Rose is a singer/songwriter from Baltimore who had been doing gigs at different Borders stores for three years. She'd never had a problem—until July 18, 2003. That's when she performed at the Borders in Fredericksburg, Virginia.

"I did the regular concert, like I normally do, which involves talking to the audience a lot," she says. "Everything was going normally, and then I said, the only statement I'm going to make about President Bush is, he's got chicken legs." That was enough to get three repeat engagements canceled.

Rose "has been banned from playing the Fredericksburg Borders Books & Music store, apparently because she made fun of President Bush's legs between songs in her show," wrote Michael Zitz, who broke the story in the Fredericksburg *Free Lance-Star*.

"I had some disconcerting feedback from the Fredericksburg store," Amy Korsun, the area marketing manager for Borders, told Rose in an e-mail three days after her performance. "There were several customer complaints about political comments that you made. . . . I am going to have to cancel all further performances at the Fredericksburg store." Rose, who had played without compensation at Borders, e-mailed back: "Your decision has upset me greatly," she wrote, and urged Korsun to reconsider.

Korsun refused. "From the feedback I have received, my decision is final," she wrote on July 22, also citing Rose for tardiness.

The Fredericksburg *Free Lance-Star* editorialized against Borders on July 26. "Borders has a very scrawny leg to stand on itself if it is wielding such a quick ax on a performer who has been perfectly suitable at other Virginia stores in the chain," it said. "If there is any place in this country where freedom of expression should get the close calls, it has to be a general-interest bookstore."

The manager at the bookstore refused to comment on the incident. Korsun was unavailable for comment. But Borders issued a statement from corporate headquarters in Ann Arbor, Michigan, after people contacted the company to complain about the axing of Rose:

We do not seek to take any political, social, or academic stance and certainly would not presume to take a stance on the issue of the President's legs. We host live music events in our stores to provide entertainment and to make the shopping experience enjoyable for our customers. Again, if political and/or social commentary is mixed in with the entertainment, we do not seek to judge the viewpoints expressed. However, the bottom line is enjoyable entertainment for our customers. In the case of Julia Rose, the quality of entertainment provided was not what the customers of that store found to be enjoyable. In fact, the staff noticed that customers were vacating the café area where Ms. Rose was performing and several customers complained, mostly about her particular style, which that evening included much more audience banter about a variety of topics than it did singing. Some did complain about her commentary regarding the President, but that was not paramount in our decision not to ask her back. . . . It was our customers' negative reaction to her at that particular store that framed our decision and caused the staff to ask that she not be invited back to Fredericksburg.

Rose disputes the claim that the audience reacted badly to her performance. Before she knew she was in trouble she had e-mailed Korsun to say, "Of all the stores I've performed in thus far, I'd have to say Fredericksburg" and one other "are my favorites, judging from crowd reaction."

"No one walked off in a huff," Rose tells me. "The thing that is so strange is that when I left that performance, I felt, wow, I did really well." One song she performed that day was "Maher's Planet," ironically about the comedian Bill Maher's own struggles with censorship after September 11. Some of her lyrics are:

This is Maher's planet,
where nobody can ban it.

Speak your mind and let it spill
Just like Bill.
Once again he's gone too far,
That's what we love about Bill Maher.

Reflects Rose: "I guess I kind of feel like Bill Maher on a smaller scale. I'm upset because I've put in over three years with these people, and I don't feel like I was treated fairly in this instance."

5. The Case of the "Seditious" Nurse—Laura Berg

Laura Berg is a clinical nurse specialist at the Veterans' Administration Medical Center in Albuquerque, where she has worked for more than fifteen years. Shortly after Hurricane Katrina she wrote a letter to the editor of the weekly paper the *Alibi* criticizing the Bush administration. "I am furious with the tragically misplaced priorities and criminal negligence of this government," she wrote. "The Katrina tragedy in the U.S. shows that the emperor has no clothes!" She mentioned that she was "a VA nurse" working with returning vets. "The public has no sense of the additional devastating human and financial costs of post-traumatic stress disorder," she wrote, and she worried about the hundreds of thousands of additional cases that might result from Katrina and the Iraq War.

Bush, Cheney, Chertoff, Brown, and Rice should be tried for criminal negligence. This country needs to get out of Iraq now and return to our original vision and priorities of caring for land and people and resources rather than killing for oil. . . . We need to wake up and get real here, and act forcefully to remove a government administration playing games of smoke and mirrors and vicious deceit. Otherwise, many more of us will be facing living hell in these times.

After the paper published the letter in its September 15–21, 2005, issue, the VA administrators seized her computer, alleging that she had written the letter on that computer. Berg responded by writing a memo to her bosses seeking information and an explanation.

Mel Hooker, chief of the human resources management service at the Albuquerque VA, wrote Berg back on November 9 and acknowledged that "your personal computer files did not contain the editorial letter written to the editor of the weekly *Alibi*." But rather than apologize he leveled a sedition charge: "The Agency is bound by law to investigate and pursue any act which potentially represents sedition," he said. "In your letter . . . you declared yourself 'as a VA nurse' and publicly declared the Government which employs you to have 'tragically misplaced priorities and criminal negligence' and advocated, 'act forcefully to remove a government administration playing games of smoke and mirrors and vicious deceit.' "

Berg was "scared for her job [and] pretty emotionally distressed," says Peter Simonson, executive director of the ACLU of New Mexico, which intervened on her behalf. "We were shocked to see the word 'sedition' used," Simonson tells me. "Sedition? That's like something out of the history books."

The ACLU of New Mexico filed a Freedom of Information Act request for documents relating to this incident. And it asked "at the very least" that Berg "receive a public apology from Mr. Hooker to remedy the unconstitutional chilling effect on the speech of VA employees that has resulted from these intimidating tactics," according to a letter from the New Mexico ACLU to the VA's regional counsel's office. Hooker refused to comment.

"While VA does not prohibit employees from exercising their freedom of speech, we do ask that such activity occurs outside government premises and not during their official tour of duty," says Bill

Armstrong, a public affairs specialist for New Mexico's VA Health Care System. "When we have reason to believe that this policy is not being adhered to, we have the obligation to review an individual's computer activity."

Senator Jeff Bingaman, Democrat of New Mexico, then took up the Berg case. "I am writing to express my deep concern regarding news reports that Ms. Laura Berg . . . was investigated for sedition after writing a letter that was critical of the current Administration," Senator Bingaman wrote to R. James Nicholson, secretary of Veterans Affairs, on February 7, 2006. "In a democracy, expressing disagreement with the government's actions does not amount to sedition or insurrection—it is, and must remain, protected speech."

Secretary Nicholson responded on March 14. "Let me be clear: Her letter to the editor did not amount to sedition," Nicholson wrote to Bingaman. "The use of the word 'sedition' was not appropriate. . . . No further action has been taken or will be taken related to the employee in this matter." Berg also had received an apology from the facility director, Nicholson said, and "appropriate action" was taken against Berg's boss, who was the one who leveled the sedition charge, he added.

"This is exactly the kind of acknowledgment we wanted to receive," says Simonson. "It provides some confirmation that activities like this weren't being broadly perceived as threats to national security, which, as preposterous as it sounds, appears to have been the mentality of at least one administrator at the VA." He praises Berg for standing up for her rights. "A lesser person would have buckled under the scrutiny or pressure, or simply not raised the issue at all."

"It's a victory," says Berg. "I'm vindicated. We still do have First Amendment rights in this country. Let's please all of us make use of them. Speak clearly and strongly."

6. *Corporate Exec Forced to Apologize for Supporting Antiwar Group—Richard Abdoo*

In 2002, Richard Abdoo was the CEO of Wisconsin Energy Corp., based in Milwaukee. That fall, Abdoo sent a $250 check to the peace group Not in Our Name. As a result he was listed as one of the thirty thousand endorsers of the group's Statement of Conscience Against War and Repression. And he was identified as "Chairman of the Board, president and CEO, Wisconsin Energy Corp." Abdoo said the donation was strictly a personal one.

The statement—signed by such celebrities as Susan Sarandon, Gloria Steinem, Ed Asner, Noam Chomsky, Danny Glover, Martin Luther King III, Alice Walker, and Kurt Vonnegut—called on "the people of the United States to resist the policies and overall political direction that have emerged since September 11, and which pose grave dangers to the people of the world." It urged people to resist "the war and repression that has been loosed on the world by the Bush Administration. It is unjust, immoral, and illegitimate." The statement condemned the loss of civil liberties in the United States, the secret detention of immigrants, and the preparation for all-out war against Iraq. (For the record, I also signed the statement.)

Right-wing talk radio jocks in Milwaukee got wind of Abdoo's endorsement and pilloried him for it. One, Charlie Sykes of WTMJ, said the statement was an "anti-American screed" and drummed up a campaign against Abdoo. "Prompted by publicity about Abdoo's contribution, 100 to 150 people . . . contacted Wisconsin Energy" in a matter of days, the *Milwaukee Journal Sentinel* reported. One longtime stockholder told the paper that he was selling his stock in Wisconsin Energy Corp. because of Abdoo's "anti-American" views. The stockholder, Laurance Newman, warned about a possible stockholders' lawsuit, and urged the company's board of directors to deal with this.

At first Abdoo stood his ground. "I think every American has the freedom to state their views," he told the *Milwaukee Journal Sentinel.* "I'd still send the $250." He seemed especially outraged at the suggestion by Sykes that he had not earned the right to criticize the United States. In his weblog entry of November 12, 2002, entitled "The Shame of Richard Abdoo," Sykes wrote:

> Amid the leftist elites who signed the statement, the presence of a prominent Milwaukee businessman is shocking enough. But more than most, Richard Abdoo has profited and thrived under the freedoms and the opportunities that others have secured for him.

Abdoo, who is the grandson of Lebanese immigrants, told the newspaper: "I'm an American. I was born here. My parents were born here. I'm proud to be an American . . . and I am really offended when someone questions my patriotism. And I'd use stronger language if I knew you weren't going to print it." But the negative comments kept coming, and the *Journal Sentinel* itself editorialized against Abdoo on November 13 in a piece entitled "An Executive's Bad Decision."

> The question is whether Abdoo, given his position and responsibilities, should have financially supported a manifesto that is so unbalanced in its condemnation of U.S. foreign policy, the Bush Administration's war on terrorism at home and abroad, and Congressional support for those policies. The answer is no.

On November 14, Abdoo backed down. In an e-mail to his employees, "Subject: Please accept my apology," Abdoo wrote:

In recent days, my personal action to support a group that advocates peace and opposes repression has been made public. I deeply regret any misunderstanding, anger, and adverse publicity that have resulted.

As much as I believed that my personal views would be separated from my position at Wisconsin Energy, I now realize that is not the case. I have learned a valuable lesson.

Please accept my apology for the distraction, confusion, and pain this situation may have caused you.

Thank you for your understanding.

7. *"My Name Is Mohamad. That Doesn't Mean I'm a Terrorist."*
—Mohamad Pharoan

Mohamad Pharoan is a waiter at the Hyatt Regency at the Inner Harbor in Baltimore. He'd worked there seven years when, on December 5, 2003, President Bush came to the hotel for a reelection fund-raiser. Pharoan, fifty-eight at the time, was supposed to be serving tables at the banquet, but he wasn't allowed to.

Because his name was Mohamad.

"When I reported to work," Pharoan says, "the whole place was under Secret Service control. They checked my name at the door, and I was standing in the hallway with my friends. My manager was talking to some Secret Service agents, and they were looking at me. Then he came up to me with worried eyes, and said, 'Is your name Mohamad?' He was my manager!"

Pharoan responded: "Of course my name is Mohamad. You know that."

According to Pharoan the manager said: "I'm sorry, you have to go home. We cannot use you today." He says his manager, with the Secret Service following, escorted him all the way to his locker, where they watched him change his clothes. "Then they showed me out the door, and I found myself in the snow."

Pharoan was born in Syria and "immigrated to the United States in 1992 and became a citizen in 1996," according to the *Washington Post*. He was not happy with how he was treated by the Secret Service. "I did what they told me, but I was extremely upset," he says. "I never complained, I never asked questions, I just said OK. But I understood it; there was no need for big brains to understand what had happened. A caveman can understand what it was about."

Pharoan then faced a dilemma: What to do? This is how he puts it: "Do I eat that shit or fight back?" He decided to consult with his brother, Dr. Bash Pharoan, who is president of the Baltimore chapter of the American-Arab Anti-Discrimination Committee.

"He said, it's up to you," Pharoan recalls. "I said, 'I don't eat shit. All my life I don't eat shit.' So he said, 'OK, let's go to the press.' "

The American-Arab Anti-Discrimination Committee issued a press release saying that it was "extremely concerned by the apparent discrimination against this individual, who is a United States citizen with no criminal record and a spotless employment history." The group also contacted the Secret Service and demanded an apology.

And it notified allies in Congress. On December 10, four members of the House of Representatives—John Conyers, John Dingell, John Lewis, and Betty McCollum—circulated a letter to their colleagues. The letter started by spoofing the MasterCard commercial:

> Price of Admission to Bush fundraiser in Baltimore: $2,000.
>
> Money Raised at Bush fundraiser in Baltimore: $1,000,000.
>
> Cost to an American citizen and seven-year hotel employee scheduled to work at the Bush fundraiser but sent home because his name was "Mohamad": Humiliation, Discrimination, and Prejudice.

The heart of the letter called the treatment of Pharoan a "monstrous form of discrimination [and a] gross violation of his civil liberties." It concluded by saying, "We cannot close our eyes to the blatant forms of discrimination that engulf the United States. We are better than this. At a minimum, we should expect our President to be as well."

One day later a Secret Service spokesperson called Pharoan and said, "We would like to apologize to you." He accepted the apology. The Secret Service also released a statement saying, "The Secret Service has apologized to Mr. Pharoan for any embarrassment or inconvenience caused last Friday when he was asked to leave the hotel. We also assured Mr. Pharoan that his exclusion was in no way related to his ethnic and religious background."

While Pharoan doesn't buy that explanation, he let the matter rest. "I made it clear that such things would not be eaten easily," Pharoan says. "I just wanted to make a point: You cannot do that to people. My name is Mohamad. That doesn't mean I'm a terrorist."

VIII

Up in the Air

1. "This Is When My Nightmare Began"—Maher Arar

Maher Arar decided to take his wife and two little kids on a vacation. So in September 2002 they left their home in Ottawa, Canada, for Tunisia. Arar was a telecommunications engineer, and while on vacation he got an e-mail from his employer at the time, Math Works, to come back early for a new client. So he booked a flight from Tunis to Zurich and—this was his mistake—to New York, before he was to fly back to Canada.

Arar was born in Syria and came to Canada when he was seventeen. He is a Canadian citizen. But that did not help him any in New York.

"My flight arrived in New York at 2:00 P.M. on September 26, 2002," he says on his Web site, www.maherarar.ca. "This is when my nightmare began." At JFK he was pulled aside while going through immigration and waited around for a couple of hours. "Then some police came and searched my bags and copied my Canadian passport," he continues in his Web site statement, from which all these quotes come. "I was getting worried, and I asked what was going on, and they would not answer. I asked to make a phone call, and they would not let me."

An FBI agent and an NYPD officer came and started to ask him questions. "I was scared and did not know what was going on," he writes. "I told them I wanted a lawyer. They told me I had no right to a lawyer because I was not an American citizen. . . . This interrogation continued until midnight. I was very, very worried and asked for a lawyer again and again. They just ignored me."

They detained him overnight.

The next day they began with more questions. "They asked me about what I think about bin Laden, Palestine, Iraq," he writes. "They also asked me about the mosques I pray in, my bank accounts, my e-mail addresses, my relatives, about everything." They held him for five days before allowing him a phone call, he says. Three days later the Canadian consul came to see him. "I told her I was scared of being deported to Syria," he says. "She told me that would not happen."

But that is what happened, even though Arar warned his U.S. interrogators that he'd be tortured there. On October 8, guards told him that the INS director had ordered his deportation to Syria. "They put me on a small private jet," he writes. "I was the only person on the plane with them. I was still chained and shackled." He was flown eventually to Rome, and then to Amman. At the Amman airport "six or seven Jordanian men" were waiting for him. "They blindfolded and chained me, and put me in a van. They made me bend my head down in the back seat. Then, these men started beating me."

Eventually, Arar was driven across the border to Syria, where things only got worse, much worse. He was placed in a building run by the Syrian military intelligence. After about four hours of questioning, guards took him into the basement. "They opened a door, and I looked in," he writes. "I could not believe what I saw. . . . It was like a grave. It had no light. It was three feet wide. It was six feet deep. It was seven feet high. . . . There were cats and rats up there, and from time to time the cats peed through the opening into the cell. I spent ten months and ten days inside that grave."

During the first two weeks guards beat him repeatedly. Sometimes they used a "black electrical cable, about two inches thick," he writes. "They hit me with it everywhere on my body." They also threatened him with electric shock and foot torture. He was forced to sign false confessions. In August 2003, he was transferred to another prison.

And finally, on October 5, 2003, the Syrian military intelligence let him return to Canada.

On November 4, 2003, he held a press conference and read the statement that I've been quoting from above.

After an outcry by journalists and human rights groups, the Canadian government agreed to hold an inquiry. The fact finder for the Commission of Inquiry, Professor Stephen J. Toope, released his report about the treatment of Arar on October 14, 2005. "I am convinced that his description of his treatment in Syria is accurate," he wrote. And Toope concluded that this treatment "constituted torture as understood in international law." He also found that "Arar's psychological state was seriously damaged and he remains fragile. His relationships with members of his immediate family have been significantly impaired. Economically, the family has been devastated."

On January 22, 2004, the Center for Constitutional Rights filed a lawsuit on Arar's behalf. It names as defendants, among others: then attorney general John Ashcroft; Larry D. Thompson, former acting deputy attorney general; Tom Ridge, the former secretary of Homeland Security; James W. Ziglar, former head of the INS; and Robert Mueller, director of the FBI. It alleges that they violated Arar's "constitutional, civil, and human rights." And in particular that they violated the Torture Victim Protection Act and the Fifth Amendment.

On February 16, 2006, District Judge David G. Trager ruled against Arar almost down the line. Judge Trager dismissed all charges relating to Arar's deportation to Syria and to the treatment he suffered there. The judge cited "crucial national-security and foreign policy considerations [that] are most appropriately reserved to the Executive and Legislative branches of government." And he carved out a huge loophole for future executive breaches:

> In sum, whether the policy be seeking to undermine or overthrow
> foreign governments, or rendition, judges should not, in the absence
> of explicit direction by Congress, hold officials who carry out such
> policies liable for damages even if such conduct violates our treaty
> obligations or customary international law.

The Canadian government took a much dimmer view. The Commission of Inquiry (commonly called the O'Connor Commission after Dennis O'Connor, associate chief justice of Ontario, who headed it) released its official report on September 18, 2006. It was scathing. O'Connor concluded "categorically that there is no evidence to indicate that Mr. Arar has committed any offense or that his activities constitute a threat to the security of Canada." And the head of the Royal Canadian Mounted Police apologized to Arar for providing inaccurate and unfair information to the Americans about him. O'Connor's report also blamed the United States for not being "forthcoming" with Canadian officials, and for sending Arar to Syria knowing the likelihood that he would face torture.

In October 2006, the Institute for Policy Studies gave its annual human rights award to Arar and his lawyers at the Center for Constitutional Rights. The Bush administration would not let him come to the United States to accept it.

On January 26, 2007, the Canadian government agreed to award Arar $9 million, and Prime Minister Stephen Harper gave him a full apology for the injustices and terrible ordeal he suffered. Harper also urged the U.S. government to remove Arar's name from any terrorist watch lists. The Bush administration refused to do so.

2. Handcuffed at the Border—Akif Rahman

Akif Rahman was born in Springfield, Illinois. Like a lot of young entrepreneurs, he went into the computer business, establishing his own consulting firm. With employees not only in the United States but also in Pakistan and India, Rahman travels a lot. And he gets hassled a lot.

Four times within a fourteen-month period, U.S. Customs and Border Protection yanked him out of lines at airports and held him for questioning. "The first time I was detained was in March 2004," he says. "I was flying back from a business trip into L.A. from Hong Kong and Pakistan. While I was picking up my bags I was asked to come to the secondary screening area." Customs agents started to drill him, asking questions like: "Why were you traveling? Who did you meet? Why were you in Pakistan? Why are you returning to L.A. and not Chicago?"

Rahman says he felt "absolutely alarmed. I didn't know what this was all about." After a couple hours, they let him go.

Five months later Rahman was returning again from a business trip to Pakistan. This time, he flew into O'Hare.

"I was met on the jetway," he says. Once again, they took him to a screening room and ran him through a similar battery of questions. "At first they were hostile, and somewhere in the middle they'd get a little kinder," he recalls. When he asked them why they were doing this to him again they said, "Just standard procedure." Rahman asked to speak to a supervisor, who told him he could fill out a Freedom of Information Act request. Rahman took the paperwork.

The very next month Rahman went to Montreal with his parents. On the way back, at the airport in Montreal, U.S. Customs officials delayed him for more than three hours. "I went through the whole drill again," he says. As a result he ended up missing his flight and a business meeting. At that point Rahman decided he better find out what was going on, so he filled out the FOIA request. "In April of '05 I got a response saying I was misidentified," he says. But that didn't prevent Customs from misidentifying him again one month later. "I was visiting my in-laws in Canada with my wife and two little kids, who were four and two at the time. We drove back across the Detroit-Windsor tunnel. Basically, I pulled up to the booth, handed them our passports, and then was told to turn off the engine and hand over the keys to the car."

Immediately, they asked him whether he had a weapon, which he didn't.

"I was walked into the border office, with two agents standing right behind me," he says. "When I went into the office I was put against the wall, with my hands up in the air. My body was searched, one of the agents kicked my feet apart, and then they handcuffed me behind my back and cuffed me to a chair."

The handcuffs hurt. "I asked the agent whether they were necessary," Rahman says. "They said this is part of the normal procedures." But this time they didn't ask him the same old questions. "I was interviewed by an un-uniformed agent from Immigration and Customs Enforcement. He asked me whether I knew someone who was funding terrorist activities or whether I knew any of the 9/11 hijackers. I felt like a suspect, like a criminal. They were asking me a bunch of questions I have no knowledge of." After more than five hours, they finally released Rahman to his wife and kids. The little ones were crying.

Rahman had had enough. "You're scared, you're frustrated, you're humiliated, you're confused, you're concerned about why it's happening and whether it will happen again. I've never been handcuffed before in my life, and who knows what's going to happen next time?"

A day or two after getting back from Canada, Rahman contacted the ACLU of Illinois. On June 28, 2005, he filed suit against the government for violating his Fourth and Fifth Amendment rights. And on June 19, 2006, he joined a lawsuit the ACLU of Illinois was filing on behalf of eight others, including his wife.

"I can't comment on the specific suit," says Bill Anthony, senior spokesman for Customs and Border Protection at the Department of Homeland Security, "but we will not let anyone in the country until we know who they say they are and that they are not here to do harm to our citizens or violate our laws."

3. Tackled on the Way to Notre Dame—Tariq Ramadan

When the University of Notre Dame invited the Muslim scholar Tariq Ramadan in January 2004 to leave his home in Switzerland and become a tenured professor in South Bend, he was excited about the opportunity.

He'd been to the United States a lot. He'd given lectures at Harvard, Princeton, and Dartmouth. And he'd spoken before the William Jefferson Clinton Foundation at an event hosted by Clinton himself in January 2002. In Europe Ramadan enjoyed a reputation as one of the leading academic voices on the Muslim world. His influential works include *Western Muslims and the Future of Islam* and *Islam, the West, and the Challenges of Modernity.* Now perhaps it was time for him to make his reputation in America.

So he accepted Notre Dame's invitation. He got a visa on May 5, 2004, and he and his family rented an apartment in South Bend. But they never lived in it.

"On July 28, 2004, a little over a week before my family and I were to move to Indiana so that I could begin teaching at the University of Notre Dame, the United States Embassy in Bern informed me by telephone that my visa had been revoked," Ramadan declares in a lawsuit he has filed against Homeland Security head Michael Chertoff and Secretary of State Condoleezza Rice. "They did not provide an explanation for the revocation at that time. On August 25, 2004, however, a spokesman from the Department of Homeland Security stated to the press that my visa was revoked because of a section in federal law that applies to aliens who have used a 'position of prominence within any country to endorse or espouse terrorist activity.' "

That federal law is the USA Patriot Act.

"I was astonished by the government's decision to revoke my visa," Ramadan says. "While I have sometimes criticized specific United States policies, I am not anti-American, and I have certainly never endorsed or espoused terrorism."

Just two days after 9/11 Ramadan wrote an open letter to Muslims that read in part:

> You know as I know that some Muslims can use Islam to justify the killing of an American, a Jew, or a Christian only because he/she is an American, Jew, or a Christian; you have to condemn them and condemn these attacks.

One month later, at a meeting sponsored by a Muslim magazine in Paris, he said, "You're unjustified if you use the Koran to justify murder." And on the first anniversary of 9/11 he was one of 199 Muslim signatories to the Statement Rejecting Terrorism. That statement said in part:

> Groups like Al Qaeda have misused and abused Islam in order to fit their own radical and indeed anti-Islamic agenda. Usama bin Laden and Al Qaeda's actions are criminal, misguided, and counter to the true teachings of Islam. . . . We call on all people of conscience to denounce violence and to work peacefully for the creation of a better world.

Interestingly enough, the government now denies that it was using the Patriot Act when it revoked Ramadan's visa. "Any statement to the contrary that may have appeared in the media or may have been made by any government spokesperson was erroneous," the government said in a court filing on March 31, 2006. Instead, it said it was using an older statute that states: "After the issuance of a visa or other documentation to any alien, the consular officer or the Secretary of State may at any time, in his discretion, revoke such visa." The government claimed that after Ramadan was issued his visa, "The State Department received information, in the ordinary course of business, that might have led to a determination that Mr. Ramadan was inadmissible."

For whatever reason, and under whatever statute, the government revoked Ramadan's visa, so he can't teach at Notre Dame. "The government's actions have caused a great deal of hardship to me and to my family," Ramadan declared. "We had hoped to make the United States our home, and we were very disappointed when that became impossible. And of course the government's actions have stigmatized me as a person. . . . Dealing with this stigma has been immensely stressful for me and for my wife and children." Ramadan said there was a societal cost as well: "My exclusion needlessly reduces opportunities for interfaith and intercultural dialogue."

That's why the American Academy of Religion, the American Association of University Professors, and the PEN American Center have joined Ramadan's lawsuit, brought by the ACLU on March 10, 2006. The revocation of his visa "has prevented United States citizens and residents from meeting with Professor Ramadan and inhibited them from hearing his views, in violation of their First Amendment rights," the lawsuit charges.

Meanwhile, Ramadan, back on September 16, 2005, applied again for a visa that would have allowed him to attend conferences in the United States. The U.S. embassy in Switzerland usually gives an answer "within 30 days of application," according to the State Department Web site, the lawsuit notes. But Ramadan was told on December 2 that "consideration of the application would likely take close to two years." On June 23, 2006, District Judge Paul A. Crotty told the government to stop stalling on this application. He said it cannot "delay final adjudication indefinitely." And he called into question the legality of excluding people on the basis of their speech. "While the Executive may exclude an alien for almost any reason," he ruled, "it cannot do so solely because the Executive disagrees with the content of the alien's speech and therefore wants to prevent the alien from sharing this speech with a willing American audience."

On September 21, 2006, Ramadan received a letter from the U.S. government with the final bit of bad news. "The State Department cites my having donated about 600 Euros to two humanitarian organizations (in fact, a French organization and its Swiss chapter) serving the Palestinian people," Ramadan said in a statement. "I donated to these organizations for the same reason that countless Europeans—and Americans, for that matter—donate to Palestinian causes: not to provide funding for terrorism, but because I wanted to provide humanitarian aid to people who are desperately in need of it."

Ramadan, who notified the State Department of his donations, believes they are a pretext. "The U.S. government's real fear is of my ideas," he writes, citing his criticism of U.S. policy in the Middle East, the Iraq War, and Bush's hostility to civil liberties. "I am saddened to be excluded from the United States. I am saddened, too, however, that the United States government has become afraid of ideas and that it reacts to its critics not by engaging them but by suppressing, stigmatizing, and excluding them."

Ramadan is now at Oxford.

4. *Greek Scholar Barred from the United States—John Milios*

Greece may be the birthplace of democracy, but a Marxist Greek professor was prohibited from entering our own democracy, thus depriving us of our right to listen to his views.

John Milios teaches political economy and the history of economic thought at the National Technical University in Athens. In January 2006, he was invited to present a paper at a conference at the State University of New York at Stony Brook. He accepted the invitation to address the June 8–10 conference, How Class Works. His visa, which he had used five times before to enter the United States, most recently in 2003, didn't expire until November 2006. But this time he didn't get in.

When he arrived at JFK on June 8 he knew something was up "from the first moment that the Border Police officer checked my passport and visa and told me that there must be some 'technical problems' with my papers," he tells me by e-mail. "The Border Police kept me in a room along with other people, mostly economic immigrants, who were also having problems with their entry into the USA." The officers suggested that his name must have gotten confused with another one that resembled his, he says.

"After five hours of waiting, I was informed by the Border Police officer that two federal agents had come to question me." Milios says they played good cop/bad cop, with one not even introducing himself and just looking angry. "They asked me two kinds of questions. First, rather typical questions related to who I am (name, age, profession, marital status, reason for traveling to the USA, etc). Second, questions about my political ideas and affiliations. They interrogated me about my public (and at least in Greece) well-known political involvement." He says they asked "to which party I belong, what the political goals of this party are, what role do I play in this party, do I belong to the leadership or not, with what means ('democratic or militant'!) are the party's goals going to be accomplished, etc."

Milios says the federal agent told him "he does not have any problem with me" and it was up to Customs. His interrogators left. At that point the Customs officer, who had been with Milios the whole time, gave him the word. He "informed me that due to technical discrepancies, my visa should be cancelled." They put him on the next flight back. "Before sending me home they photocopied everything that I had in my wallet (including credit cards), and they took my fingerprints from all ten fingers," he says.

Milios is outraged at his treatment. "I find the whole incident ridiculous. Who is afraid of my research work and ideas? Why should overseas Marxist research not be discussed with American citizens in the USA? I am startled and astonished!"

Lucille Cirillo is a spokesperson for Customs and Border Protection. "Based on information provided by the State Department, Milios was determined not to be admissible into the United States," she says.

"This seems to be another instance of ideological exclusion," says Jameel Jaffer, deputy director of the ACLU's national security program. "The Supreme Court has repeatedly held that the First Amendment protects not only the right to speak but the right to listen." He cited former Supreme Court justice William Brennan in *Lamont v. Postmaster General*, who said, "It would be a barren marketplace of ideas that had only sellers and no buyers."

For his part, Milios wants to return to the United States. "I am very eager to come back," he says. "I have a lot of good friends and colleagues in the USA, and I also want to participate in at least two scientific conferences in the near future."

5. Grounded by No-Fly List—Peace Action Milwaukee

Alia Kate, sixteen, a high school student in Milwaukee, wanted to go to Washington, D.C., on April 20, 2002. She was looking forward to demonstrating against the School of the Americas and learning how to lobby against U.S. aid for Colombia. She had an airplane ticket for a 6:55 P.M. flight out of Milwaukee on Friday the nineteenth, and she got to the airport two hours ahead of time.

But she didn't make it onto the Midwest Express flight.

Neither did many other Wisconsin activists who were supposed to be onboard. Twenty of the thirty-seven members of the Peace Action Milwaukee group—including a priest and a nun—were pulled aside and questioned by Milwaukee County sheriff's deputies. They were not cleared in time for takeoff and had to leave the next morning, missing many of the events.

"I was one of the first people in our group to try to check in," says Kate. "When I went up to get my boarding pass, the lady said there were some problems. She said her computer had locked up and she had to wait for someone else. And I found out that the someone else was one of the sheriff's deputies on duty. And the sheriff's deputy came and told me I had to grab my bags and follow her for further questioning." Kate was "a little scared," she says. "I was alone and was taken to a building nearby. They had my driver's license. I heard them making phone calls, reading off some stuff on my license." She says she grew more concerned when they asked her what her nationality was.

"I said I'm half Persian and Italian and German.

"They asked who was Persian, my mother or my father.

"I said, my father, my biological father. I don't even know him.

"They also asked me if I was a U.S. citizen.

"I told them I was.

"They asked me if I was from around here.

"I said yes."

Finally, they walked Kate back to the ticket counter.

"They gave us our boarding passes, which had a bold-faced S with little asterisks on both sides, circled with an ink marker," Kate says. "This meant that when we went to the gate our carry-on bags would have to be hand searched and they'd have to wand us." But the deputies took so much time going through the whole group that not everyone was ready to go by 6:55.

Midwest Express held the flight for as long as it could but then left, almost empty, without most of the activists. Sister Virgine Lawinger also was detained. "When I went through the line the lady at the ticket counter said, 'I'm sorry, you have to wait a minute,' and then the sheriff's deputy came and took me and some others to an office," she says. "They said our names were flagged. That's the real strange thing: What caused the computer to flag those names? I did feel it was profiling a particular group without a basis—a peace group."

Father Bill Brennan of St. Patrick's Church in Milwaukee also missed his flight because of the questioning. "No one was advised of his or her civil rights," he says.

Sarah Backus, another peace activist, says she was told by one of the sheriff's deputies: "You're probably being stopped because you are a peace group and you're protesting against your country." Backus later asked the sheriff, David Clarke, about this, and he denied this was the reason for the detentions. She also went to the Midwest Express ticket desk to find out what was going on. "The names are in the computer, and the names came up," she was told. What tripped them up was the computerized "no-fly list" that the federal government now supplies to all the airlines but at the time was unknown to the public. The airlines are required to check their passenger lists against that computerized no-fly list.

"The name or names of people in that group came up in a watch list that is provided through the federal government and is provided for everyone who flies," says Sergeant Chuck Coughlin of the Milwaukee sheriff's department. "The computer checks for exact matches, similar spellings, and aliases. In this particular case there were similar spellings. About five or six individuals came up on the watch list. Although it was time consuming, and although they were flight delayed, the system actually worked."

Don't tell Dianne Henke that. A volunteer with Peace Action, Henke is the person who organized the whole trip. "We were very upset," she says. "Here we were, going out to lobby, to use our democratic rights, to talk to our legislators, to use our freedom of speech and dissent, and then we're being detained and not told why. We were taking young people and telling them if you use means that are nonviolent and peaceful, your message will be heard. But the fact that we were hampered, that we were detained, was just a totally different message."

6. "Please Step Aside"—Rebecca Gordon and Jan Adams

On August 7, 2002, two peace activists, Rebecca Gordon and Jan Adams, were detained by police at the San Francisco airport. Gordon and Adams, veteran peace and justice activists in the Bay Area, work on a newspaper called *War Times*.

"We get to the airport at nine thirty in the evening for an eleven thirty flight to Boston," Gordon tells me. "As we go to the check-in counter, the woman takes our IDs and types in our names, and then says, 'There's something wrong with my computer.' So she goes and gets another woman, who types our names into her computer. She, too, says, 'There's something wrong with my computer. Please step aside so we can check the other people in.' "

Gordon says she and Adams thought there might be a problem with their e-tickets. But it was more serious than that, as they found out a few minutes later when one of the airline employees told them, "You both turned up on the FBI no-fly list, and we've called the San Francisco police. They are coming over to talk to you. In the meantime, one of us has to stay with you, so please come along with your baggage," Gordon recalls. She says the woman from the airlines seemed bewildered. "We were standing there in the middle of the airport, and I'm sure she's thinking these are just garden-variety middle-aged white dykes."

"I can't imagine why this is happening," the airline employee said, according to Gordon. "And I said, 'Well, I can tell you why. We work on a paper that opposes the war on terrorism.' Her eyes got kind of big, and she said, 'Oh.' "

Three uniformed members of the police then came, took their IDs, and called headquarters. They wouldn't even let her get a drink of water. "After ten or fifteen more minutes one of the officers told us, 'You aren't on the master list,' and they handed us back to the airline," Gordon says.

But the airline was still suspicious, and circled a big S on their boarding passes. "I assume it means search, and then a red S was put on it," Gordon adds. "In fact, at the gate we were selected for search, and they did the usual search procedure, the wanding and the shoes. Before I got on I asked the ticket agent if this is going to happen every time. She said, 'I don't know, but I'd recommend that you get to the airport early.' "

For its part, the San Francisco police has little comment. "Whenever anyone comes up on the no-fly list we come out in one or two minutes and the situation is cleared up," says Larry Ratti, a spokesperson for the police at the airport.

Ratti says the department gets calls about suspicious people at the airport "maybe one a day, one every two days." Some of these calls come from the no-fly list, "but we don't differentiate," he says. "It's just a suspicious-type-person call."

In April 2003 Gordon and Adams, along with the ACLU of Northern California, sued the Transportation Safety Administration and the FBI, which were refusing to release information about the no-fly lists. "We are deeply concerned about the government's secret watch lists and the lack of government accountability," said Adams at the time of the filing. "We want to find out how our names appeared on a government watch list, and how we can get our names off the list. But instead of answering our questions, the federal government has refused to release any information."

In January 2006, the government settled the case by agreeing to pay $200,000 in legal fees to the ACLU of Northern California. As a result of their action Gordon, Adams, and the ACLU of Northern California say they were able to pry loose some crucial information.

"We brought the lawsuit because we believe the public has a right to know about the 'No Fly' list and other government watch lists," said Adams in a press release issued by the ACLU of Northern California. "And we succeeded in doing so by making public hundreds of pages of documents that not only confirmed the existence of the 'No Fly' list, but exposed many of the serious problems with the list." One of those was that the government admitted that the criteria for placing people on the list were "necessarily subjective."

The no-fly list grew from sixteen on September 11, 2001, to one thousand a year later, the documents revealed. According to its press release, the ACLU of Northern California believes the list now contains "tens of thousands of names."

7. U.S. Rowing Champion Snagged on No-Fly List—Aquil Abdullah

Aquil Abdullah has been called the Jackie Robinson of rowing.

He was the first African American to win the title of U.S. national champion in the single scull in 1996.

He was a silver medalist at the 1999 Pan Am games.

He became the first African American to win the diamond scull at the Henley Royal Regatta in 2000, one of the oldest and most prestigious races in the world.

He won the U.S. rowing championships in 2002.

He was on the U.S. Olympic rowing team in 2004. He and his partner, Henry Nuzum, reached the finals and set an American record.

But to the Transportation Security Administration Abdullah was just another black man with a Muslim-sounding name, and therefore a suspect.

Three times, he was detained at airports. "The first time it happened it wasn't too bad," he says, recalling an incident in late 2001. "When I went to board my plane I was asked to step aside. They notified the airport police officers, who came around asking me questions. I thought it was weird, since I was flying with a U.S. passport and had a driver's license. But at the same time I knew security was an issue."

After this incident Abdullah thought he'd be in the clear. "Now they've checked me out, I'm cool, they're going to put my name into a database and say this guy's all right," he remembers thinking. But that's not what happened. A few weeks later Abdullah was trying to catch an early morning flight from Lake Placid, New York, where he was training, to Seattle, to participate in an international competition and to give a speech. "I missed my flight because, when they pulled me aside, there was no one around," he says. "The officers who were supposed to verify my identity weren't even there yet. At that point I was a little perturbed. I'm a pretty low-key guy. But I was upset. I was talking to one of the police officers about it. He completely sympathized with me; he said it was ridiculous. He said he had to run a check on this two-year-old boy. Basically, it was just name profiling."

Abdullah said they held him for an hour and a half. "I was late," he says. "I didn't do well in my race."

The third time he was detained Abdullah was trying to fly from Newark to Seattle in early 2003 when he was pulled out of line again. "Anyone with a common Muslim name has to be checked out, to see if it's an alias, to see if he's on a terrorist list," Andrew Kurpat, a police officer with the Port Authority in Newark, told Ira Berkow of the *New York Times*, who broke the story.

Abdullah stresses that he understands "there was a definite need for security. The thing is true: Terrorists only need to succeed once. We've got to find out the problem every time. But at the same time, we could have been more intelligent about it. It would have been a lot easier to create a database that says this is the same Aquil Abdullah with this passport number and this address" whom we've already checked out.

The irony of his situation was not lost on Abdullah. "Here I was representing my country as an athlete, doing my best to show what the United States was all about," he says, "and my country couldn't even figure out that I was a citizen. It made me a little sad."

IX

A Course in Campus Surveillance

1. Terrorism Task Force Comes to Drake—Brian Terrell

Brian Terrell is the executive director of the Catholic Peace Ministry in Des Moines, Iowa. On November 15, 2003, he participated in a conference at Drake University called End the Occupation, Bring the Iowa Guard Home, and he helped organize a nonviolent protest the next day at the National Guard's local headquarters.

On February 4, 2004, law enforcement officers arrived at his office before he did. "I got a call that a detective with the Joint FBI Terrorism Task Force was here to serve me papers," he recalls. Jeff Warford of the Polk County Sheriff's Department left his card, which mentioned that he was with the task force.

Elton Davis was issued a subpoena also. A member of the Catholic Worker community in Des Moines, which practices nonviolence and service to the poor, Davis returned to his home one day in early February only to find "the subpoena was taped to my door. It was kind of scary."

The prosecutor, U.S. attorney Stephen Patrick O'Meara, subpoenaed two others: Patti McKee, coordinator of the Iowa Peace Network, who gave a nonviolent training at the Drake conference, and

Wendy Vasquez, a local Quaker and antiwar activist who visited Iraq in 2002. The prosecutor also served papers on Drake University, which for a while couldn't even discuss the issue. "There is a federal gag order," said Linda Ryan, senior assistant to the president of Drake. "We can't talk about it."

The university was even ordered to turn over documents about who attended the conference, which was sponsored by the local National Lawyers Guild. And the university was ordered to identify the leaders of the local guild chapter. The university did not furnish the material. And the National Lawyers Guild, along with other civil liberties and peace groups, raised an outcry. "We see this as an attempt to intimidate and further silence any dissent and criticism of the government's policies," said Heidi Boghosian, executive director of the National Lawyers Guild at the time.

On February 9, 2004, O'Meara's office released a statement that said in part, "The United States Attorney's Office does not prosecute persons peacefully and lawfully engaged in rallies which are conducted under the protection of the First Amendment to the Constitution of the United States." Under public pressure, the federal prosecutor withdrew the subpoenas before the month was out.

By the way, it turns out that not just students and peace activists attended the End the Occupation conference at Drake. At least two Polk County sheriff's deputies infiltrated it. "On November 15, 2003, this Senior Deputy Leo along with Senior Deputy Griffiths, both acting in an undercover capacity, attended a Civil Disobedience workshop held at the Olmstead Center at Drake University," reads a law enforcement document that the protesters obtained. The document, on the stationery of the Mid-Iowa Narcotics Enforcement Task Force, is entitled "Anti-War Protest."

"It's just really rude" to have undercover agents present during antiwar meetings, says Terrell, whose name was mentioned in the document. "One was supposed to get arrested with us. We trust people. We take people at face value. I'm just disappointed in these two people as human beings."

2. Army Goes to UT Law School—Sahar Aziz

Sahar Aziz was a third-year law student at the University of Texas Law School in Austin in February 2004 when she organized a campus conference on Islam and the Law: The Question of Sexism. "It was nothing out of the ordinary for a law school conference," she says. "It was an academic conference discussing the sociological, political, historical, and legal perspectives."

The press release announcing the event was hardly eye-opening:

> This conference addresses a variety of issues where Muslim women's rights in Islam facially appear to be compromised by Islamic Law. This interdisciplinary conference aims to discuss and analyze these issues in a balanced manner. . . . The objective is to reveal the complexity of Islamic Law through the different scholarly interpretations on the same subject matter. In contrast, the conference is not meant to support a certain interpretation or school of thought, nor to be a venue for religious propaganda.

But for some reason the conference caught the eye of two army lawyers based at Fort Hood, Texas, who attended the conference. "We didn't know there was any army personnel there," says Aziz. "No one was in uniform. There was no one who identified themselves as being with the army. The optimistic view is they were there to learn. The pessimistic view is they were there to spy. We don't know."

The army takes the optimistic view. The army lawyers attended the conference to "help prepare them for their assignments in South-west Asia, where they will deal with legal issues between the American Forces and the largely Muslim populace," says a March 12 press release from the U.S. Army Intelligence and Security Command. At the conference the army lawyers took a grilling from at least one person attending the conference. They "were persistently questioned about their identity, occupation, and status by a man who appeared to be attending the conference with two associates," the latter press release says. "The tone and repetition of the questions made the army lawyers suspicious. They subsequently reported the matter to local military intelligence officials."

And so the army came snooping around. "On February 9, two U.S. Army counterintelligence special agents went to the law school to request a roster of attendees in an attempt to identify the suspicious individual and his two associates."

One of the agents was Jason Treesh, special agent, Army Intelligence. "He was looking for me," says Aziz, who has Treesh's card, which he left in her box at the law school. "He knew I was the main organizer. He basically went from office to office asking where I was." Friends contacted her, telling her: "Someone is looking for you, and you should be careful."

"I was freaking out," Aziz recalls. "I was very stressed, thinking, 'Oh, my God, I can't believe this!' You kind of wrack your brain and wonder how the conference might have ignited such scrutiny." Other law students were also rattled, she says. "People were intimidated, to say the least. He was not in uniform, but he was flashing his badge around and looking for a roster and a video recording." He never received either.

Fearing he would come to her home with a warrant or a subpoena, Aziz called her attorney, Malcolm Greenstein, who ascertained that

Aziz herself was not in trouble. "Why is the military doing domestic surveillance?" he asks.

Douglas Laycock, associate dean of research at the University of Texas Law School, agrees that the army did not have jurisdiction to come on campus. "We think they overreacted," he adds. "It cannot be that everybody who attends an academic conference becomes a suspect." A little while later the army itself admitted it had overstepped its bounds. "The special agents and their detachment commander exceeded their authority by requesting information about individuals who were not within the Army's counterintelligence investigative jurisdiction," said a statement of the U.S. Army Intelligence and Security Command. "To prevent this from happening again, INSCOM has provided refresher training on the limits of Army counterintelligence investigative jurisdiction to all counterintelligence personnel performing duties in the United States."

But not everyone is reassured. Will Harrell, the executive director of ACLU of Texas, doesn't buy the whole story. He believes that the army lawyers who attended the conference did so with the full knowledge of their superiors. "It was a direct attempt to stifle dissent on that campus. It worked! Students are still traumatized over there. Others are terrified about what this means, and they're wondering whether they're on some list somewhere. I don't care if it's FBI or army intelligence. The aim is the same: to intimidate."

As for Aziz, the presence of the army at her conference cast a pall. "I'm very disappointed," she says. "They rained on my parade. Here was this conference that was very successful and that I had worked hard to put together, and then suddenly it was like something straight out of the movies." The experience only cemented her fears. "I thought my own concerns as a Muslim about civil rights were exaggerated. But wow! This is confirmed. This country is changing."

3. *A Date with the Secret Service at Durham Tech—A.J. Brown*

A.J. Brown was a freshman at Durham Tech in North Carolina in the fall of 2001. On October 26, she got a knock on the door. "It was five on Friday, and I was getting ready for a date," she says. When she heard the knock she opened the door. But it wasn't her date.

"Hi, we're from the Raleigh branch of the Secret Service," two agents said, she recalls. "And they flip out their little ID cards, and I was like, 'What?' And they say, 'We're here because we have a report that you have un-American material in your apartment.'" Incredulous, Brown denied the charge.

"Are you sure? Because we got a report that you've got a poster that's anti-American," they told her. Brown again said no. They asked if they could come into the apartment.

"Do you have a warrant?" Brown asked. "And they said no, they didn't have a warrant, but they wanted to just come in and look around. And I said, 'Sorry, you're not coming in.'" One of the agents told Brown, "We already know what it is. It's a poster of Bush hanging himself," she recalls. "And I said no, and she was like, 'Well, then, it's a poster with a target on Bush's head,' and I was like, nope."

The poster they seemed interested in was one that depicted Bush holding a rope, with the words: "We Hang on Your Every Word. George Bush, Wanted: 152 Dead." The poster has sketches of people being hanged, and it refers to the number who were put to death in Texas while Bush was governor, she explains.

Ultimately, Brown agreed to open her door far enough so that the agents could see the poster on the wall of her apartment, though she did not let them enter. "They just kept looking at the wall," which contained political posters from the Bush counterinaugural, a Free Mumia poster, a picture of Jesse Jackson, and a Pink Floyd poster with the quotation "Mother, should I trust the government?"

At one point in the conversation one of the agents mentioned Brown's mother, saying, "She's in the armed forces, isn't she?" (Her mother was, in fact, in the army reserve.) After they were done inspecting the wall one of the agents "pulled out his little slip of paper, and he asked me some really stupid questions, like my name, my Social Security number, my phone number," she says. "Then they asked, 'Do you have any pro-Taliban stuff in your apartment, any posters, any maps?' I was like, 'No, I don't, and personally, I think the Taliban is just a bunch of assholes.' "

With that, they left. They had been at her apartment for forty minutes.

"This sounds like one of our protective intelligence cases, and we do not discuss our protective intelligence cases," says Kimberly Bruce, a spokesperson for the Secret Service.

"They called me two days later," says Brown, "to make sure my information was correct: where I lived, my phone number (hello!), and my nicknames."

4. UMass–Amherst Economics Professor Gets FBI Visit
—M.J. Alhabeeb

Professor M.J. Alhabeeb teaches economics at the University of Massachusetts at Amherst. But when two campus police officers, one working for the FBI, came to pay him a visit on the afternoon of October 24, 2002, they weren't interested in discussing his microeconomic theory of the family or signing up for one of his courses on small-business finance.

"They came to my office and said they were acting on a tip someone called in saying I am anti-American," he recalls. "I asked, 'What does that mean?' And they said, 'You are opposing the president's pol-

icy on Iraq.' And I said, 'Millions of Americans are opposing the war.
What's the big deal?' "

The officers also asked, "When did you come here? And when did
you become a citizen?" he says.

Alhabeeb fled Iraq in 1982 and is now a U.S. citizen, according to
the *Boston Globe*, which broke this story. He "rarely discusses politics
even with his friends," the *Globe* reported. "He felt compelled to prove
his loyalty to the United States by explaining [to law enforcement]
that his brother-in-law, a lawyer in Iraq, was executed" by Saddam
Hussein's regime. Alhabeeb, who himself was harassed in Iraq because
he was not a member of the Baath Party, says the visit from the officers
"does bring back bad memories. I should live a different life, not similar to the one I lived before." He thinks the visit resulted from a
grudge. "Someone wanted an opportunity to hurt me.

"This specific visit was not a horrible thing by itself," he says, but
he is concerned about "the indiscriminate questioning of people based
on ethnicity, religion, or color, and the threat to academic freedom and
civil liberties. If we feel that we have to be cautious, that we have to
hold our thoughts—this should never become the norm in American
society."

When I asked the FBI to comment on this, a spokesperson, Gail
Marcinkiewics, said, "This was the least intrusive way of figuring out
what was going on."

Faculty members at UMass–Amherst, as well as the ACLU of
Massachusetts, are suspicious of FBI snooping on campus and dis-
trustful of campus police doubling as FBI agents. On December 12,
2002, the ACLU of Massachusetts filed a Freedom of Information Act
request with the FBI. "The enlistment of campus security officers to
serve the intelligence interests of the FBI within the academic community raises concerns for First Amendment freedoms," the group
said. It is seeking all records after September 11, 2001, dealing with

"FBI cooperation or liaison with campus police or security officers at colleges and universities in the United States for the purposes of gathering intelligence and/or investigating students, faculty, and/or employees of the college or university."

Bill Newman is the director of the western Massachusetts office of the ACLU. "The presence of the FBI dedicating significant resources to investigations on a university campus imposes an enormous chilling effect on academic freedom, robust debate, and political dissent," he says. "Absent legal law enforcement purposes, the presence of the FBI would constitute an anathema to freedom of inquiry for which a university must stand."

5. Pentagon Spies on Santa Cruz Peace Group—Kate Flanagan

"It was our first big event as a group," says Kate Flanagan, a member of the University of California–Santa Cruz's Students Against War (SAW). Flanagan was referring to the April 5, 2005, antirecruitment action the group pulled off, which the Pentagon itself was monitoring, unbeknownst to SAW. "We decided we were going to make the recruiters leave campus," says Flanagan, who was a freshman at the time.

Chanting slogans like "Racist, sexist, antigay, hey recruiters go away," about 270 students arrived at the building where the career fair was being held. SAW was able to get about 70 students inside the building, and eventually the recruiters did leave. "There was no confrontation," she says. "We were having a teach-in inside. We wanted it to be a hate-free campus. We had a speak-out afterward that gave all students the mic if they wanted it. A couple of counterdemonstrators talked, too."

On December 14, 2005, MSNBC did a story entitled "Is the Pentagon Spying on Americans?" NBC then posted a chart the Pentagon had been keeping on a variety of actions, including SAW's. The chart listed the event as a "threat" and characterized the threat as "credible."

Flanagan said she and other group members took it in stride. "It was kind of validating almost to show that what we were doing was important, and they were scared about what we were doing, which showed we had the power to disrupt the normal state of affairs," she says. "We were aware of the spying on activists in the sixties and seventies, so we weren't surprised that the government was spying on us. Everyone else was a lot more shocked than we were."

SAW got more creative the next time military recruiters were on campus, which was October 18, 2005. The group decided to stage a kiss-in. "About twenty-five or thirty of us went in to talk to the recruiters. We just pretended that we were really interested," she says. Then, a little while later, "twelve pairs of students lined up in front of the recruiters and made out for an hour and a half. The recruiters kind of sat back and sexualized what was going on, making comments about lesbians."

The kiss-in prevented the recruiters from doing their work. "It ended really well," says Flanagan. "We did a conga line out of the building, chanting, 'Recruiters off our campus.' " She says the group does not know whether the Pentagon was spying on the kiss-in or not.

SAW, with help from the Northern California ACLU, is suing the Pentagon to force it to release documents related to the spying. "We've already got some back that showed they had been on our Yahoo listserv," says Flanagan. "You wouldn't know how to get on unless you'd been to a SAW meeting."

On April 11, 2006, SAW held another counterrecruitment action. Conservative columnist Michelle Malkin blogged about it, writing, "UC Santa Cruz Hates Our Troops." She also listed the phone numbers the group had posted for press contacts, and death threats came in by phone and by e-mail.

Here are a couple, taken from SAW's Web site, www.saw .revolt.org:

"You will pay for your seditious activities. It is only a matter of time. . . . We are retired military snipers & we are watching you."

"My sincere hope is that a couple hundred of the local patriots take a day off work for your next anarchist event, and come down to your little shithole with some axe handles and bust your fucking heads."

Another person wrote that he hopes "a fine young American very, very soon puts his shiny barrel up to your left temple and pulls the trigger. Now THAT will make America a much, much better place to live for the rest of us, you utterly disgusting piece of shit."

8. Cop Makes Midnight Raid of Teacher's Classroom—Tom Treece

Tom Treece was giving one of his favorite courses, called Public Issues, at Spaulding High School in Barre, Vermont, in the spring of 2003 when he became a public issue himself. It all began after a local police officer entered his classroom under peculiar circumstances in the dark of night.

The uniformed police officer, John Mott, went into the class at about one thirty on the morning of April 9, 2003. He told the *Times Argus* that he "entered the school through an unlocked maintenance door." The school superintendent, Dorothy Anderson, says he banged on the front door of the school and got the custodian to let him in.

In any event, he convinced the custodian to unlock the door to Treece's classroom. Mott took a picture of a student's poster that showed President Bush with duct tape over his mouth. The poster carried the words "Put your duct tape to good use. Shut your mouth." Treece told me this project was part of an assignment for a unit he was teaching on Iraq. It had three parts:

The first part was to participate in a debate on whether to invade Iraq.

The second was to write a paper defending your perspective on the issue.

And the third was to make a poster illustrating your point of view.

Six of his students put together the offending poster.

Mott, who did not return several calls from me, told the *Times Argus*, "I wanted everybody else to see what was in that room." The paper said the students' project "offended him as an American and a retired military man." He told the paper, "Having spent 30 years in uniform, I was insulted. I'm just taking a stand on what happens in that classroom as a resident and a voter and a taxpayer in the community."

Mott, incidentally, used to work at Spaulding High as the JROTC officer.

Superintendent Anderson disapproved of Mott entering the school during off hours to further his own political agenda. "I find this behavior, at the very least, in violation of our policy for visitors at the school," she wrote Police Chief Michael Stevens on April 16.

> I also find it disturbing that a police officer would wear his uniform under such circumstances, thereby intimidating our employee into letting him in the building at a very unusual hour. I question the intent of his visit. Why could he not have come during regular school hours? Please look into this matter and determine if any ethical or legal guidelines were breached.

According to Anderson the police chief told her "he was going to handle it administratively." Stevens did not return several phone calls.

On his radio show Rush Limbaugh called Mott a hero and posted the students' artwork on the Limbaugh Web page. Anderson was not happy about that. "These kids didn't turn these projects in with any understanding that they would end up on Rush Limbaugh," she said. "Their parents feel very violated and angry."

X

Student Suppression

1. Girl, Fifteen, Suspended for Protest Shirt—Katie Sierra

Katie Sierra was a fifteen-year-old sophomore at Sissonville High School in West Virginia when September 11 hit. That fall may not have been the easiest time to form an anarchist club. But that's what she tried to do. On October 22, 2001, she notified her principal, Forrest Mann; he denied her request. It was the only club he had ever disallowed, according to the lawsuit Sierra and her mother filed against the school.

Sierra had already made up flyers for the club, which she wasn't able to distribute. The flyers said: "Anarchist club. Anarchism preaches to love all humans, not just of one country. Start a newspaper, a food-not-bombs group, a book discussion group. Speak your point of view, and hear others. Please join." The next day Sierra came to school wearing a T-shirt that said "Racism, Sexism, Homophobia, I'm So Proud of People in the Land of the So-Called Free." The principal suspended her for three days. "I've never been in trouble before," Sierra says. "I was kind of upset at first: How could he? Then I was crying. How could he suspend me for something so ridiculous as that?"

On October 29, she was told that before she could come back to school, she would have to provide the principal with authorization to obtain her medical records, she would have to meet with a school psychologist, and she couldn't wear T-shirts like the one she wore or organize her anarchist club.

At a school board meeting that night the president, Bill Raglin, allegedly said, "What in the hell is wrong with a kid like that?" Another school board member, John Luoni, accused her of treason, according to her court papers.

To make matters worse, says Sierra, Mann mischaracterized her T-shirt in the *Charleston Gazette,* falsely stating it included statements such as "I hope Afghanistan wins" and "America should burn." As a result students at school ganged up on her. "I got shoved against lockers," she says. "People made pictures of me with bullet holes through my head and posted them on, like, the doors in the school. They said some really harsh things. It was scary."

Sierra and her mother sued the school district but lost in the lower courts and in the state supreme court by a 3 to 2 vote. "We sought an injunction to force the principal to allow her to form the anarchy club and wear her peace T-shirts and void her suspension," her attorney, Roger Forman, says. Forman, a former president of the West Virginia ACLU, says her free speech rights have been violated.

Because she felt unsafe at Sissonville High, Sierra opted to be homeschooled.

2. High School Junior Prevails with "International Terrorist" T-shirt
—Bretton Barber

One day when Bretton Barber was a junior at Dearborn High School in Michigan, he decided to make a statement. And then he made a statement about making a statement.

On February 17, 2003, he wore a T-shirt that had a picture of Bush on it and the words "International Terrorist." At lunch, another student complained to a vice principal, Michael Shelton, about the shirt, and a teacher also worried about its appropriateness, says Barber.

Shelton told Barber to turn the shirt inside out or go home. Barber chose the latter option.

The principal, Judith Coebly, later told Barber that he couldn't wear the shirt again at school. School spokesman Dave Mustonen told CNN that though the school recognizes that students have the right to freedom of expression, the administration was concerned about the tense atmosphere over the issue of the imminent Iraq War. "It was felt that emotions are running very high," Mustonen said.

Barber decided to fight the decision and went to the Michigan ACLU. "It's a gutsy thing for a high school student to take on a school administration in this way," said Kary Moss, executive director of the ACLU of Michigan, in a press release.

> It's obvious that Bretton feels very strongly about this issue, and we want to make sure that his ability to express his political opinion isn't hindered in any way. I'm hoping that we can resolve this issue without going to court. However, if the school is unwilling to allow students the right to political expression, we'll have no choice.

The school was unwilling, so Barber and the ACLU of Michigan filed suit one month later for a permanent injunction against the banning of the shirt. They won. "Students benefit when school officials provide an environment where they can openly express their diverging viewpoints and when they learn to tolerate the opinions of others," District Judge Patrick J. Duggan ruled.

"This ruling is an important civics lesson for students everywhere," said Andrew Nickelhoff, the ACLU of Michigan cooperating attorney who argued the case. "Sometimes we must have the courage—as Brett Barber did—to defend our rights." Barber mostly just wanted to get his antiwar message out. "It's especially important," he said, "for students who may be asked to fight at some point to have the right to say how we feel."

3. Secret Service Previews High School Talent Show— *Boulder High School, Colorado*

It's not out of the ordinary for high school kids to form a band. And so when a group calling itself Coalition of the Willing rehearsed for the annual talent show at Boulder High School in November 2004, you wouldn't expect the Secret Service to take an interest. But it did.

Somehow the Secret Service found out that Coalition of the Willing was rehearsing an old Bob Dylan tune called "Masters of War." The last stanza of the original includes the lines: "I hope that you die and your death will come soon./I'll follow your casket in the pale afternoon."

According to the *Daily Camera* of Boulder, some students alleged that at one of the rehearsals the band changed the language to "George Bush, I hope that you die. . . ." That allegation reached a talk radio show in Boulder, which spread it far and wide. Lead singer Allysse Wojtanek-Watson adamantly denies that anyone mentioned Bush's name on stage. "The only singer who had a mic was me, and I never said anything like that in the slightest," she tells me. "I never did it in rehearsal, I never did it in band practice, and I never did it at the performance. I've never threatened the president in my life." The school principal, Ron Cabrera, backs her up. The accusation was "unfounded and untrue," he told AP.

Nevertheless, the Secret Service came to the school on November 11 and "questioned him for 20 minutes and took a copy of the group's song lyrics," the AP reported. The Secret Service also questioned a teacher who was advising the group. November 11 was an unusual day for Wojtanek-Watson. "I was walking through the halls," she says, "and someone yells, 'You communist.' Another person said my name was on the radio. There were news crews all over the place. And then someone told me the Secret Service was looking for me."

She couldn't believe it. "I was extremely stunned," she says.

Lon Garner of the Secret Service confirmed to the *Daily Camera* that agents had visited the school and that the investigation was ongoing. "We are very sensitive to the First Amendment rights, but we still have to investigate allegations of threats, regardless," he told the paper. Lorie Lewis, a spokesperson for the Secret Service in Washington, D.C., was aware of the investigation and told me the agency "investigates every potential threat to its resolution."

The Secret Service did not attend the talent show on November 12, according to the *Daily Camera*.

The talent show itself, and the singing of the Dylan song, went off without incident, the paper reported. "It's all really ridiculous," Wojtanek-Watson says. "It was a huge overreaction. I can't see what all the hubbub was about."

4. FBI Talks to Muslim High School Student About "PLO" Jottings—Munir Mario Rashed

Munir Mario Rashed was a sixteen-year-old junior at Calvine High School in Sacramento in the fall of 2005 when two FBI agents came to the school to question him. "I was scared," he told the *Los Angeles Times*. "I didn't know what was going on or what I had done wrong."

Evidently, what he had done wrong was to scribble the initials PLO on his binder—two years earlier.

At that time he had gotten into an argument with his math teacher.

Rashed, a fourth-generation Palestinian American, had defended the PLO, while the teacher called it a terrorist group, according to the Lawyers' Committee for Civil Rights of the San Francisco Bay Area. On September 27, 2005, the FBI agents asked about the PLO and "whether he had pictures of suicide bombers stored on his cell phone," the *Times* reported. "He told agents that the only photo he carried on his phone's screen was of a mosque."

On December 15, 2005, the Lawyers' Committee and the Sacramento Valley office of the Council on American-Islamic Relations issued a statement alleging that the school district had violated its own policy during this incident:

> Administrators at Calvine High School apparently violated a school board policy that requires a student's parents be informed whenever a law enforcement officer requests an interview on school premises. [In a private room] the agents asked the student to recount an incident that had occurred two years earlier in a math class. He told the agents that his teacher had reprimanded him for having scrawled the letters "PLO" on his binder. The teacher said that anyone who supported the PLO was a terrorist.

Shirin Sinnar, an attorney at the Lawyers' Committee, says: "The FBI should not be interviewing kids about their political views, and schools should not be short-circuiting the involvement of parents in such a frightening situation." In a December 15 letter Sinnar sent to the president of the Elk Grove Unified School District she urged the district to

take appropriate disciplinary action against Calvine High School administrators for failing to notify Munir's parents, [and to] investigate whether any school official at Elk Grove High School was
responsible for reporting Munir to the FBI and take appropriate disciplinary action.... If any school official was responsible for the
"tip" to the FBI, such an action would constitute a deprivation of
Munir's right to free speech in the school setting.

The school district issued a statement on December 15 responding to the letter. "The district is investigating the allegations raised in
the letter and, as appropriate, will deal with the issues. The district re-
alizes the importance of the rights of all the parties involved, including those of law enforcement." It has since been trying to resolve the
matter and has changed its policy, says Elizabeth Graswich, public information officer for Elk Grove Unified. "The new policy says that
when law enforcement comes in, school officials should make every
reasonable attempt to notify the parent guardian at the time the law
enforcement requests to interview any student regarding any non-
school-related legal investigation."

The FBI confirmed that its personnel visited the school and interviewed the student, saying they did so "as a result of information received from a complainant," according to a statement released by the
FBI's office in Sacramento. "The complainant alleged the student had
written 'PLO' on a binder and had pictures of suicide bombers on his
cell phone. Information concerning possible terrorist or threat activity, however benign, is reviewed by the FBI."

It also says that its agents gave Rashed the opportunity to contact
his parents. "Prior to the start of the interview, the student was asked
by the agents if he wanted a parent present and was told he did not
have to answer any questions," the FBI statement says. "The student
indicated he would discuss the interview with his parents later."

According to the FBI statement the questioning took about twenty minutes, and at the end the agents decided not to pursue the matter further. "The issues brought forth by the complainant were resolved, and no further action has been taken," the statement says.

Rashed, who did not return my phone calls, has reportedly suffered adverse reactions. "The entire experience left the student badly shaken," says the December 2005 joint statement from the Lawyers' Committee and the Council on American-Islamic Relations. "He has since been hesitant about expressing his political views in any context."

5: *Wal-Mart Turns In Student's Anti-Bush Photo, Secret Service Inspects—Currituck County High School, North Carolina*

Selina Jarvis is the chair of the social studies department at Currituck County High School in North Carolina. For her senior civics and economics class in the fall of 2005, she told students "to take photographs to illustrate their rights in the Bill of Rights," she says. One student "had taken a photo of George Bush out of a magazine and tacked the picture to a wall with a red thumb tack through his head. Then he made a thumb's-down sign with his own hand next to the president's picture, and he had a photo taken of that, and he pasted it on a poster."

According to Jarvis, the student, who remains anonymous, was just doing his assignment, illustrating the right to dissent. He went over to the Kitty Hawk Wal-Mart to get his film developed. An employee in that Wal-Mart photo department called the Kitty Hawk police on the student. And the Kitty Hawk police turned the matter over to the Secret Service.

On Tuesday, September 20, 2005, the Secret Service came to Currituck High. "At one thirty-five, the student came to me and told me that the Secret Service had taken his poster," Jarvis says. "I didn't believe him at first. But they had come into my room when I wasn't there and had taken his poster, which was in a stack with all the others." She says the student was upset. "He was nervous, he was scared, and his parents were out of town on business."

She, too, had to talk to the Secret Service. "Halfway through my afternoon class the assistant principal got me out of class and took me to the office conference room. Two men from the Secret Service were there. They asked me what I knew about the student. I told them he was a great kid, that he was in the homecoming court, and that he'd never been in any trouble."

Then they got down to his poster. "They asked me, didn't I think that it was suspicious," she recalls. "I said no, it was a Bill of Rights project!" At the end of the meeting they told her the incident "would be interpreted by the U.S. attorney, who would decide whether the student could be indicted," she says. The student was not indicted, and the Secret Service did not pursue the case further.

"I blame Wal-Mart more than anybody," she says. "I was really disgusted with them. But everyone was using poor judgment, from Wal-Mart up to the Secret Service." A person in the photo department at the Wal-Mart in Kitty Hawk said, "You have to call either the home office or the authorities to get any information about that." Jacquie Young, a spokesperson for Wal-Mart at company headquarters, did not provide comment. Sharon Davenport of the Kitty Hawk Police Department said, "We just handed it over" to the Secret Service. "No investigative report was filed."

Jonathan Scherry, spokesperson for the Secret Service in Washington, D.C., said, "We certainly respect artistic freedom, but we also have the responsibility to look into incidents when necessary. In this case, it was brought to our attention from a private citizen, a photo lab employee."

Jarvis uses one word to describe the whole incident: "ridiculous."

6. *Student Antirecruiter Arrested—Tariq Khan*

Tariq Khan used to be in the air force. At twenty-seven, he was old to be a junior at George Mason University in Virginia in the fall of 2005. And he wasn't one to hold back on his strong views about the Iraq War and military recruitment on campus. He went to the trouble of making up his own antirecruitment pamphlet, which he entitled "Three Good Reasons Not to Join the Military." Those reasons, he says, are: first, you have to submit to authoritarianism; second, you have to commit human rights violations; and third, you have to risk your own life for leaders you might not respect or trust. Khan says he has kept these pamphlets with him on campus because he's never sure when the recruiters will be there.

And so on September 29, when he saw the U.S. Marine recruiters had set up a table in the Johnson Center on campus, Khan decided to stand nearby. "I got out an 8½-by-11 piece of paper, which I had written on: 'Recruiters Lie. Don't Be Deceived.' And I taped it to my chest," Khan says. "I was standing about four feet from the marine recruiting table. I wasn't blocking access or anything." Khan says that someone from the Johnson Center staff came up to him and told him he couldn't be there.

"He kept telling me that I had to have a permit to 'table,' " Khan says. "But I told him I wasn't tabling. I don't need a permit just to stand there."

"Do you want me to call the police?"

"Call whoever you want, but I'm not leaving."

Then Khan says a student came by, took a pamphlet, ripped it up, threw it in his face, and left. The student returned with another person, who said he was in the marines and was just back from Iraq. Khan says he asked him, "How many people did you kill?"

The marine said: "Not enough. I want to go back and kill more."

They started to hassle Khan, calling him "a pussy and a coward," he recalls. "The guy who said he was in the marines rips the sign off my chest. I said, 'Thanks for defending my freedom of speech.' So I took out another piece of paper and started to make a new sign." Soon a campus police officer, Theodore Reynolds, showed up.

"He told me the same thing: that I'm not allowed to be there unless I have a permit. I told him I don't need a permit to stand here." When Khan wouldn't leave Reynolds allegedly threw him down and handcuffed him. Khan says that some of the students nearby were egging the officer on, yelling, "Kick his ass! Kick his ass!"

Khan says he kept saying, "I'm nonviolent. I've committed no crime."

Reynolds and another police officer allegedly dragged Khan out and took him to the George Mason University police station. There they found out his name. (Khan is a Pakistani American who was born in the United States.) "All of a sudden they started talking about 9/11," he says. "They said, 'You people are the most violent people in the world. There's no telling what you'll do.' "

The officers then took him to the Fairfax Adult Detention Center. Reynolds allegedly said: "If you run your mouth off again, or even look at an officer the wrong way, they'll hang you up by your feet." Khan was charged with trespassing and disorderly conduct, and after about an hour he was let go. He faced up to two years in jail and a $5,000 fine.

The ACLU of Virginia defended Khan. "The kind of political speech in which Tariq was engaged goes to the core of the First Amendment," says Rebecca Glenberg, legal director of the ACLU of Virginia. "We find it quite alarming that a student could be arrested on his own public university campus for expressing a political position. The very purpose of a university is to encourage open debate and the free exchange of ideas."

Khan's arrest created a stir on campus. On October 3, there was a protest to support him, and campus police were videotaping the demonstrators, according to the *Washington Post.* On October 5, there was a teach-in. And 129 faculty members signed a letter calling for a review of the police conduct, as well as of the school's policy on free speech, the *Post* said. A petition signed by 443 students, faculty, staff, alumni, and members of the community urged the university to "drop all charges." It also called upon the "campus police to account for and destroy the videotaped surveillance which took place" at the October 3 protest.

The university, under pressure, ultimately decided to recommend that the DA drop the charges, and that's what happened on the morning of November 14. "We're strong, strong proponents of free speech," Daniel Walsch, director of media relations at George Mason University, says, adding that the university was conducting its own internal investigations.

"This arrest should never have occurred," said Kent Willis, executive director of the Virginia ACLU. "Mr. Khan stood quietly in a public place expressing his opposition to actions taken by our government. This is precisely the kind of expression the First Amendment was designed to protect."

7. Muslim American Running Back Sacked from Team— Muammar Ali

The 2005 football season was supposed to be Muammar Ali's year at New Mexico State University, predicted *Sports Illustrated.* In its NCAA football preview, it wagered that "Muammar Ali, who led the team with 561 yards rushing, will get even more opportunities." But on October 9, he "received a message on his phone answering machine at his home that his jersey was being pulled and that he was released," says a letter from his attorney, George Bach, of the ACLU of New Mexico, to the university.

That letter, dated October 25, alleges that head coach Hal Mumme engaged in religious discrimination. "Coach Mumme questioned Mr. Ali repeatedly about Islam and specifically, its ties to Al-Qaeda," the letter states. This made Mr. Ali uncomfortable. And then, after the team's first game, "despite being the star tailback for several years, Mr. Ali was relegated to fifth string and not even permitted to travel with the team." There were only two other Muslim players on the team, the brothers Anthony and Vincent Thompson, and they were also released. The letter adds that the coach "regularly has players recite the Lord's Prayer after each practice and before each game."

Ali's father, Mustafa Ali, says the trouble started at a practice over the summer when the coach told the players to pray. "My son and two other players who were Muslim, they were praying in a different manner, and the coach asked them, 'What are you doing?' They said, 'We're Muslims. This is how we pray.' That had a lot to do with how things went south." Mustafa Ali says things escalated after his son had a personal meeting with Coach Mumme in which the coach "questioned him about Al-Islam and Al-Qaeda." His son talked to him about the conversation. "He told me it was very weird," Mustafa Ali recalls. "It disturbed him quite a bit. He didn't understand why it had anything to do with football."

After that meeting the coach "never spoke to my son again," Mustafa Ali says. "And as they moved into summer camp football my son noticed that he wasn't getting the ball as much and wasn't playing as big a role."

This surprised Mustafa Ali. "In 2004, he was honorable mention All-American in his sophomore year. He was the fastest, strongest, quickest person on the team." His son "just knew there was something wrong."

When his son got cut "he was upset, he was upset. The coach never gave a reason. None." I asked to speak to his son, but Mustafa Ali said that would not be possible. "He's not talking to the media at this time. He's a very shy person."

I asked the university whether I could talk to Coach Mumme. Tyler Dunkel, director of athletic media relations for New Mexico State, said, "No way." The Associated Press reported that Mumme had apologized to the team in November 2005 for any unintended insults.

The university hired an Albuquerque law firm to look into the allegations. That firm, Miller Stratvery, cleared the university. It "found that the players were released from the team based on their performance and attitudes, not because of religion," according to AP. Peter Simonson, executive director of the ACLU of New Mexico, "questioned the impartiality of the probe."

On August 28, 2006, the ACLU of New Mexico sued New Mexico State on behalf of Ali and the Thompson brothers, alleging religious discrimination and violations of the athletes' religious freedom.

"Universities are supposed to be places of evolved thinking and reason, not of base intolerance and bigotry," says Simonson. "Being coach doesn't give someone the right to make a football team into a religious brotherhood."

"We did nothing wrong, and we deny the allegations," said Bruce Kite, general counsel for the university. "It's a garbage lawsuit," added Bob Gallagher, a New Mexico State regent.

8. *Muslim American Students Kicked Off Bus—Jacksonville, Florida*

On October 29, 2003, Fort Caroline Middle School in Jacksonville, Florida, let out like any other day. But one of the bus rides home was hardly typical.

According to the students an angry bus driver kicked about twenty-five Muslim kids off and made them walk five miles home. "I was like sitting in the middle of the bus, the lady who was driving was so mad at the people in the back," says Sara Kazim, who was thirteen. "I didn't hear them yelling or doing something bad. But she stopped the bus, and she started yelling at us, and she told the Muslims to get off the bus." This was during Ramadan, so they were fasting, which made the walk home all the more difficult. "We were so tired and thirsty, and our legs were hurting."

Zahra DiyaaAldeen was another student on the bus. She says the bus driver wouldn't even let them talk. "All of a sudden she came up to the girls who were wearing the scarves, she was pointing at us, 'You, you, you, get off the bus.' She was saying bad words, like 'F___ you, you son of a ___.' She was treating us like animals." DiyaaAldeen says there was an African girl who was Muslim but who wasn't wearing a scarf, and she wasn't kicked off.

The walk home was difficult and frightening, she says. "We were so far away." At one point DiyaaAldeen approached a house and knocked on the door and asked to use their phone. The woman who answered the door said something racist, and "she slammed the door in our face. . . . Our moms were crying so bad" when they got home, she says.

The Florida chapter of the Council on American-Islamic Relations (CAIR) called for an investigation. "The school district needs to send a clear message that anti-Muslim bigotry will not be tolerated," said Parvez Ahmed, chair of CAIR-FL.

The attorney general of Florida investigated the allegations that the bus driver "violated Muslim students' civil rights and unlawfully interfered with same when she instructed, directed, and otherwise forcibly removed only visibly Muslim students from a First Student, Inc., school bus and made derogatory statements about Muslims after

driving away from Fort Caroline Middle School," according to a settlement agreement with the bus company. In that agreement First
Student denies that the driver "acted in a discriminatory manner toward the Muslim students." It maintains that "the Muslim students'
conduct posed a threat of imminent danger" to the driver. "Accord-
ingly, she was justified in . . . refusing to drive the students home."
First Student "makes no admission of liability and none should be in-
ferred," the agreement states.

The agreement requires the company and its employees to obey
Florida laws prohibiting discrimination; to adopt a policy "concerning
unlawful harassment and discrimination in the transportation of students"; to provide training to its employees; to make a $10,000 dona-
tion to Communities in Schools of Jacksonville; and to pick up $26,885
in attorneys' fees and costs incurred by the attorney general's office.

"They didn't give us nothing," says DiyaaAldeen. This incident, as
well as harassment at school, affected her a lot. She got tired of people
saying, "Your daddy is Saddam Hussein or Osama bin Laden," or, "You
are terrorists."

She has since dropped out.

XI

Teacher, Beware

1. Student Teacher Canned for Teaching About Islam—
Stephen K. Jones

Stephen K. Jones, thirty-four, was a graduate student at the University of Maine at Orono, where he was looking to get his teaching degree. As part of his program he was required to do a twelve-week internship. In the spring of 2002 the administrators placed him at Old Town High School and Middle School, though he never did get to the middle school.

For his tenth-grade high school class on world history, Jones developed a lesson plan on Islam and Islamic civilization. He says that the university approved it ("I got an A on that"), as did the principal and the tenth-grade world history teacher, Marty Clark, whose class he would instruct.

March 1, 2002, was Jones's first full class. "The very first thing I did was ask, 'What do you think Islam is?'" he says. And his students responded with the following words: "crazy, terrorist, uneducated, poor, dirty, oppresses women."

"I wrote all those things on the board, and I said we're going to take a look at these depictions, and we're going to see what are some other ways to look at Islam, Muslims, and Islamic civilizations," he says he told the class, which "seemed to go OK."

But at the second class "people began to get worked up when I said let's look at the various monotheisms—Judaism, Christianity, Islam." Jones provided excerpts from the Torah, the Gospel of Matthew, and the Koran, and he asked the students, in a handout, to consider the following questions:

Who is God?

What happens to those who are not faithful to God and who break the rules?

What is the purpose of life?

How does God wish to be worshipped?

How are family and society valued?

The next day Clark told Jones he had gotten a call from a parent, who said Jones was trying to convert her kid to Islam, Jones recalls. "A couple days after that, the principal wanted to see me, because of a few more calls from parents." At the end of the day on Friday, March 8, Jones met with the principal, Terry Kenniston, and offered to meet with the parents. "Don't worry about it," Kenniston said, according to Jones. "I don't see a problem. A few phone calls does not put this on the top of our agenda here." Jones says Kenniston's "feet were up on the desk, he was leaning back, and he didn't seem all that concerned."

Then, on the following Monday, after teaching a class and overseeing a study hall, Jones saw his adviser, Ruth Townsend from the University of Maine, approach.

"You are in deep doo-doo," she told him.

"Well, what does this mean?"

"Basically, they don't want you here."

Jones says he was shocked. "I expected something, like, 'You're going to have to meet with the parents, or with the superintendent,' or, 'We're going to have to change your teaching plan,' or, 'Marty is

going to have to teach it with you.' Not, 'You're going to have to
leave the building.' That's what really blew my mind." The next
morning "I stopped by my office to collect my stuff, and Marty said
the superintendent doesn't want me to teach anywhere in Old Town,"
Jones says.

Later that day Jones had a meeting with the superintendent, the
principal, Townsend, and Anne Pooler, the associate dean for teacher
instruction at the college. "They wanted me out, and that was that,"
recalls Jones. "But they would put nothing in writing, and they
wouldn't spell out the exact reasons why I was not tenable there." At
that point Jones notified the local newspapers.

Once he did that the dean of the College of Education and Human
Development, Robert Cobb, told him he would not authorize another
student-teaching placement for him, and informed Jones that he had
no legal rights in this matter. Jones was kicked out of the master of
arts in teaching program. "I don't have the emotional or financial
wherewithal" to sue the school district, he said, "and that's how these
folks usually win. It takes so much energy to fight."

Marty Clark and the principal at Old Town High School refused
to return several phone calls. The superintendent of the Old Town
School District, Owen P. Maurais, told me, "I'm going to refer you
with any question you have to the University of Maine. That's all I'm
going to say. He's a student at the University of Maine, and they have
jurisdiction to talk about this matter."

Dean Robert Cobb said, "I regret to tell you that it's against our
policy to comment on individual students and their performances."
Dean Cobb later faxed over a March 15 statement. It said, "Issues sur-
rounding a University of Maine student internship are unfortunately
causing perception problems for one of the University's most valued
educational partners."

Jones expressed concerned about the lesson his students might have drawn from the experience. "If you're not popular, or say something that not everyone approves of, you can be out of a job," he says. "So the lesson they learn is: Obey. It's sick."

2. English Teacher Loses Job over Iraq War Digression—Elizabeth Ito

Elizabeth Ito came to the teaching profession late. She made the career shift when she was thirty-six. "When I discovered teaching, I thought, wow, this is where I'm going to stay," she says. After working as an adjunct English instructor for five years, she was hired by Forsyth Technical Community College in Winston-Salem, North Carolina. "When I got this job, I remember saying to one of my colleagues, I'm going to retire from Forsyth Tech."

But she no longer works for Forsyth Tech. The school administration refused to renew her contract because, she says, she spoke out one day in class against the Iraq War.

The date was Friday, March 28, 2003. "I spent ten minutes at the beginning of my business-writing class . . . in an impromptu and sharply worded critique of the war in Iraq," she wrote in an account on the Web. "Two students notified my supervisor . . . that I had been criticizing the war in class." The following Monday her supervisor, along with the dean of the College of Arts and Sciences, John Slade, met with Ito for two hours. They told her that "war was not pertinent to the curriculum I was hired to teach," she wrote. "At the end of the meeting, Dean Slade asked me to promise not to raise the topic of the war again in class. I told him that while I had no intention of revisiting the topic, I was unwilling to make such a promise. He replied, 'That's insubordination.' " A few days later Slade sent Ito a disciplinary letter that said, in part: "Should you choose to abuse again the authority you hold over your students in the manner you did on March 28, the response and any resulting disciplinary action may be more severe than a written warning."

Ito says she didn't discuss the war again in class, but on May 15 she received a letter saying that Forsyth Tech was not rehiring her. "They said they fired me for deviating from the curriculum, but it was only ten minutes, so I can't believe that every teacher who has deviated from curriculum for ten minutes ends up fired," she says. "They're distinguishing the content of my speech. That's why I maintain I was fired for political reasons. I also contend that talking about the war for ten minutes, even in an English class, is not inappropriate simply because the war is such a momentous current event."

Gary Green, president of Forsyth Tech, gave me his side of the story. "This is not a situation that's about freedom of speech, academic freedom, politics, or the war," he says. "It's not about a single incident. It's about a teacher who was not doing her job adequately. She had a probationary status her first year, and we made the decision that we thought was in the best interest of our students and the college."

Ito says that before March 28, however, she received four positive evaluations. "Then I criticized the war, and then I got my annual review that covers the same period of time, and it was overwhelmingly negative," she says. "That just tells me I was persecuted for what happened that one day in my class."

With a lot of support from the local peace and justice community, she pursued her case through university channels, with two administrative appeals hearings in the fall of 2003. After her first appeals hearing, on October 8, the school dropped its claim that she had failed to perform her duties as an instructor competently or professionally. All it maintained at the end, she says, was that she had behaved in an unprofessional manner toward her class on March 28; that she was insubordinate in not agreeing to attend a meeting that she actually had attended; and that she had a bad attitude with supervisors. "The Committee is convinced that your political views were neither a basis nor a reason for the non-tendering of your contract," it said.

At the second hearing, on December 18, she read a statement to the board of trustees. "My teaching contract with Forsyth Technical Community College was not renewed for political reasons, specifically, for my opposition to the war against Iraq," she said. "That was the end," she says later, explaining that North Carolina is a right-to-work state. "All they had to do was follow their own preestablished procedures. I never had a chance."

She still finds the administrators' position "very disingenuous," she says. "They claimed the content of my speech didn't matter, just the deviation from the curriculum. But we all know that professors will talk about sports for ten minutes at the beginning of class."

Being let go by Forsyth Tech took a toll. "It really did seriously damage my career, and it hasn't fully recovered," she says. In June 2006, Ito moved to Spain to try to find a teaching job there.

3. Antiwar High School Teachers Punished—Albuquerque, New Mexico

To be a freethinking high school teacher in New Mexico when George Bush was dragging the nation into the Iraq War was a perilous occupation.

On March 11, 2003, Carmelita Roybal, who teaches ninth-grade English at Rio Grande High School in Albuquerque, was suspended for two days without pay when she did not take down her No War Against Iraq sign. Heather Duffy, who teaches art at the school, hung a similar sign the next day in solidarity with Roybal and she, too, was suspended.

On March 13, "45 students walked out of class" to support the teachers, the *Albuquerque Tribune* reported. The students "were videotaped by school officials and likely will be cited for truancy. . . . School police arrested four students when they refused to go to class."

On March 19, Ken Tabish, a guidance counselor at Albuquerque High School, was suspended for refusing to take down antiwar material he had posted in his office, including a copy of a speech by Senator Robert Byrd. "I am a person of peace, and in good conscience, I cannot take them down," he said. So Tabish was put on administrative leave and lost two days' pay.

Also on March 19, Francesca Tuoni, a language teacher at Albuquerque High who is the adviser to a campus group called Students for Participatory Democracy, was ordered by a vice principal to remove a flyer on her classroom wall that advertised a peace rally. Tuoni complied with the order.

Meanwhile, at a third school within the same district, two other teachers got into similar trouble. At Highland High Geoffrey Barrett and Allen Cooper "have been placed on leave for refusing to remove war-related student artwork posted in their classrooms," the AP reported. "Barrett, who teaches history and current events, said the student art carried both anti-war and pro-war messages, and was created as part of a class assignment." Cooper, who teaches English, had one antiwar sign up "by an Afghani student who has had family members killed in U.S.-led bombings in Afghanistan, he said."

Cooper and Barrett were suspended for two days without pay.

On April 18, the American Civil Liberties Union of New Mexico sued Albuquerque Public Schools and several administrators for violating the rights of Roybal, Cooper, and Tabish. The suit says that the plaintiffs' First and Fourteenth Amendment rights were violated. According to the suit the district was apparently under pressure from members of the Albuquerque community to crack down on unpatriotic sentiments. The Rio Grande High School principal "called Roybal into his office and retrieved a piece of paper from his trash can to show her. It was a photocopy of a photograph of her poster, with an anonymous note attached that stated the following, verbatim: 'I want this removed now!! She cannot push her political agenda in the school—she has been & continues to badmouth our President, our country, and conservatives. It stops now!!' " (The quote was in all caps, and the last line was underlined twice.) Albuquerque High School counselor Tabish also got into trouble "because an anonymous parent had complained."

The superintendent of the Albuquerque Public Schools, H. Thomas Garrity II, defended the school's policy prior to the suit by saying, "Recent personnel actions taken by APS have been the result of insubordination to reasonable requests to provide an atmosphere free from bias and prejudice." Administrators also quoted from the teachers' contract, which states: "The teacher will serve as an impartial moderator and will not attempt, directly or indirectly, to limit or control the opinion of pupils on controversial issues."

But the suit says "there is no evidence" that the plaintiffs "directly or indirectly attempted to limit or control the opinion of students" with regard to the Iraq War, and that "plaintiffs have never created an atmosphere of bias and prejudice."

"There has to be a space for free speech for teachers," says Peter Simonson, executive director of the ACLU of New Mexico. "And we're trying to carve out an appropriate space for that."

Carve it out they did.

On November 14, 2003, the ACLU of New Mexico reached a settlement with the school district and declared victory. "We couldn't have hoped for a better outcome," said Simonson in a statement. Cooper, Roybal, and Tabish got back pay and the removal of their letters of reprimand. The school district agreed to pay their legal fees, and the school agreed that in the future it would go to mediation before suspending employees for speaking out on controversial issues.

4. Poetry Teacher Slammed, Slams Back—Bill Nevins

Bill Nevins taught humanities at Rio Rancho High School near Albuquerque from August 2001 to June 2003. One of his assignments, he says, was to reinvigorate the extracurricular writing programs at the school. So he started the Rams Slam Poetry Team and the Write Club. Student interest grew.

"In December 2002, we had a phenomenal poetry event at school," he recalls. "About 80 percent of the school attended over the course of the day." Nevins brought in some of the leading poets in the state, many of them Native American, Chicano, or black, and he had students do their own readings, too. He says one administrator said: "This is the most dynamic thing I've ever seen at this school."

After that Nevins encouraged his students to perform in coffeehouses and bookstores. And since school clubs were invited to publicize their events as part of the daily announcements on the school's closed-circuit TV, some of Nevins's students took it upon themselves to read a poem or two and encourage everyone to join up or come to a reading.

That's how Nevins got in trouble.

Shortly before Bush launched the Iraq War one of Nevins's students, Courtney Butler, read her poem "Revolution X" as part of an announcement: "You drive by a car whose bumper screams God Bless America./Well, you can scratch out the B and make it 'Godless' because God left this country a long time ago."

"The next day I knew there was a problem," Nevins says. "The assistant principal was very upset. She interrupted my class and demanded a printed copy of the poem." Nevins didn't have one, so she asked the student's father, who was also a teacher at the school, to go home and get it. He refused.

The assistant principal also said Larry Morrell, the guidance counselor, was making a "terrible stink." Morrell, Nevins says, refers to himself as the school's military liaison and "issued an e-mail demanding to know who had authorized this subversive speech." Morrell also sent an e-mail to the principal saying that whoever authorized the poem should be "horsewhipped," according to a document discovered during the lawsuit Nevins filed against the district.

After that the principal issued a memo that said that nothing could be read publicly at school unless it had been submitted to him ten days ahead of time with all the controversial parts underlined. "I did object to that," Nevins recalls. "We were planning another, larger poetry gathering, and I'd invited Rudolfo Anaya, and I said it would be very awkward to have Mr. Anaya underline his remarks. I asked for a meeting, but he never responded."

His response became clear, however, on March 17, 2003.

"With no warning at all, an assistant to the principal came into my class, the last one of the day, and said, 'Bill, you need to go to the principal's office; I'm taking over your class.' So I went to the principal. When I got there he said, 'You're placed on administrative leave with pay while we investigate the situation.'" The next day Nevins was called into the superintendent's office, where he was told he "had not properly filled out forms for students to go on field trips," Nevins says. "This was bogus." At a subsequent meeting school officials told him his contract was not going to be renewed. "They didn't give cause," he says. "They cited their discretion."

The decision to let Nevins go was controversial. Students protested against it, and there were several large rallies in New Mexico supporting him. Nevins filed suit on September 14, 2003, against the school district, accusing it of violating his free speech rights. In July 2004, the school district settled the lawsuit for $205,000. It admitted no wrongdoing.

"The decision to settle this matter is by no means an admission of guilt on the part of Rio Rancho Public Schools," the district said in a statement on August 2, 2004. "The district remains firm that Mr. Nevins's First Amendment rights have never been violated . . . Rio Rancho Public Schools stands by its decision not to renew Mr. Nevins's contract based on personnel issues. The district settled the case on the advice of its attorneys and insurers solely based on the mounting costs of litigation."

Nevins claims victory, though. "We used some of that money," he says, "to make a film record of what happened, and to set up a non-profit, the Poetic Justice Institute, to encourage free speech and poetry among youth."

5. Teacher Told Not to Mention "Peace" in Class—Deb Mayer

Deb Mayer was a teacher of fourth, fifth, and sixth graders at Clear Creek Elementary School in Bloomington, Indiana, during the 2002–2003 school year. On January 10, 2003, she was leading a class discussion on an issue of *Time for Kids*—*Time* magazine's school-age version, which the class usually discussed on Fridays, and which is part of Clear Creek's approved curriculum. Several articles in the magazine discussed topics relating to the imminent war against Iraq, and one mentioned a peace march.

According to Mayer, a student asked her if she would ever participate in such a march. Mayer recalls responding: "When I drive past the courthouse square and the demonstrators are picketing, I honk my horn for peace because their signs say, 'Honk for peace.' " She says she added that she thought "it was important for people to seek out peaceful solutions to problems before going to war, and that we train kids to be mediators on the playground so that they can seek out peaceful solutions to their own problems."

"It didn't dawn on me that people would object to me saying peace was an option to war," Mayer tells me. "I didn't even think it was controversial."

But it sure turned out to be.

"One student went home to tell her parents that I was encouraging people to protest the Iraq War," she says. "The parents called the principal and demanded to have a conference. The dad was complaining that I was unpatriotic. He was very agitated. He kept rising out of his chair and pointing his finger at me and yelling, 'What if you had a child in the service?' I said, 'I do have a child in the service.' "

At the time, one of Mayer's sons was a naval nuclear engineer aboard the USS *Nebraska*, she says, adding that he's now an officer in Afghanistan. She told the parent, Mark Hahn, that her son also "doesn't preclude peace as an option to war. And that made him even angrier. At the end of the meeting Hahn insisted that the principal, Victoria Rogers, make Mayer refrain from talking about peace again in the classroom. "I think she can do that," Rogers responded, according to Mayer. "I think she can not mention peace in her class again."

"I was just floored," Mayer says, "but I said OK because we had a parent out of control, and I didn't want to be insubordinate. I thought that would be the end of it."

It wasn't.

At the end of that day Rogers circulated a memo, entitled "Peace at Clear Creek," that said: "We absolutely do not, as a school, promote any particular view on foreign policy related to the situation in Iraq." And she canceled the annual "peace month" that the school had been holding.

At the end of the spring semester the school district did not renew Mayer's contract, and she and Michael Schultz, her attorney, allege that this was in retaliation for her political expression. In her pending federal lawsuit she says that the school chilled her First Amendment rights because of one conversation in a class, which she says took up all of about five minutes.

"This is a classic First Amendment free speech case," says Schultz. "It involves, for the first time as far as I can tell, the right of a teacher to express an opinion in a classroom while teaching approved curriculum."

The school district, the Monroe County Community School Corp., takes a different view. While neither Rogers nor anyone at the school district would respond to my phone calls, the district mounted an aggressive legal defense. Represented by the law firm of Locke Reynolds in Indianapolis, the district sought summary judgment, asking the judge to throw out the case.

"Ms. Mayer's one-year contract was non-renewed after ongoing parent complaints about her and her teaching style, and five students being transferred out of Ms. Mayer's classroom at the parents' request," says the brief for the school district. And it summons affidavits from parents finding fault with Mayer's teaching style. The brief does not deny that the Iraq War discussion took place, or that the Hahns got upset by it. In fact, it acknowledges that Mayer was instructed to refrain from discussing her opinions on the war. But the brief says that during the parent conference on the subject, "according to Principal Rogers, Ms. Mayer was borderline unprofessional." And it states further that the Hahns alleged that Mayer continued to talk about the war in class, a charge she denies.

The gist of the district's case, as outlined in its brief, is this: "Ms. Mayer's speech on the war was not the reason for her ultimate termination. Instead . . . the motivating factor for her termination was her poor classroom performance, the ongoing parental dissatisfaction, and the allegations of harassment and threats towards students."

Schultz, in his court filing in response to the request for summary judgment, rebuts this argument. He says the affidavits about poor performance are pretexts. They "were signed in the summer of 2005, more than two years after Plaintiff's termination. . . . Those alleged complaints about Ms. Mayer were not and could not have been relied on by Principal Rogers in making her decision to terminate Plaintiff's contract with the school." He also cites an evaluation that Mayer received that had praised her effusively.

Mayer says that at one time the school district did offer to settle—for $2,500. She had already spent ten times that amount, so she refused it. Plus, she wants to defend the free speech rights of teachers.

On March 10, 2006, District Judge Sarah Evans Barker dismissed Mayer's case, granting summary judgment to the defendants. The judge said that the school district was within its rights to terminate Mayer because of various complaints it had received from parents about her teaching performance.

Beyond that, Barker ruled that "teachers, including Ms. Mayer, do not have a right under the First Amendment to express their opinions with their students during the instructional period." The judge added that

> school officials are free to adopt regulations prohibiting classroom discussion of the war, [and that] the fact that Ms. Mayer's January 10, 2003, comments were made prior to any prohibitions by school officials does not establish that she had a First Amendment right to make those comments in the first place. . . .
>
> Whatever the school board adopts as policy regarding what teachers are permitted to express in terms of their opinions on current events during the instructional period, that policy controls, and there is no First Amendment right permitting teachers to do otherwise.

The judge has given enormous leeway to school districts to limit teachers' speech in the classroom, and "has simply gotten the law wrong," says Schultz. "There is a long line of authority that teachers do not check their First Amendment rights at the schoolhouse door. And, in this case, Ms. Mayer was asked for her opinion in the context of teaching the approved curriculum. She only gave her opinion in a very appropriate, limited way, and then related the issue to the students' lives (i.e., on the playground), and then moved on in the lesson. If giving one's opinion in response to a legitimate (and predictable) question is fair game for making a decision to terminate a teacher, who will want to teach? And, more importantly, what impact will this state of affairs have on the quality of instruction?"

Mayer is concerned about the bad precedent this decision sets. "Teachers everywhere are at risk," she says, "because of what this judge has said."

The case has cost Mayer dearly, she adds: "I have lost my house, my income, my health insurance, my life savings, and my prospects for employment." She is appealing.

6. Catholic High School Teacher Refuses Flag, Forced Out— Stephen Kobasa

Stephen Kobasa takes the Gospel seriously. For twenty-five years he taught at Catholic schools, spending the last six teaching English at Kolbe Cathedral High School in Bridgeport, Connecticut.

But he gave that job up in the fall of 2005 because he could not abide having an American flag in his classroom. "Everything in the Gospel rejects what flags stand for: boundaries, hatreds, creation of enemies," Kobasa says. "For a Catholic Christian school that holds up the crucifix as a symbol of God's love, the flag can only be a contradiction. The Church can only function with its prophetic voice by standing outside the state."

Over the years, whenever he found an American flag in his classroom he removed it, he says. That never caused a problem before. But then a new policy came down in August 2005 from the board of education at the Bridgeport diocese: the school day would begin with a prayer and a pledge of allegiance.

Kobasa, who is part of the extended nonviolent community of the Hartford Catholic Worker and Jonah House in Baltimore, knew he would have trouble abiding by that. He hoped to negotiate some compromise. "I met with the principal, and she said she was aware that I had not been doing the pledge, but that now there would be a problem because it was the policy," he recalls. "So what I offered was an arrangement by which any students who wanted to make this oath of fealty could do so with a flag that they could have available. But only for the duration of the pledge itself, and then the flag would once again be removed."

The principal, Jo-Anne Jakab, went along. "She agreed to that. So I thought that was the end of it. Ten days later I was called down to her office, at which point she announces that this compromise, which she thought would be acceptable, is not." The superintendent of schools, Dr. Margaret Dames, warned that "if I refused to accept the policy, that would be taken as an indication that I no longer wished to work for that school system."

Kobasa said he decided to accept the decision "under protest and under duress," and he filed a grievance with his schoolteachers' association.

In his classroom he attached two quotations to the flagpole. One was from Paul's Letter to the Galatians: "There is neither Jew nor Greek, there is neither slave nor free person, there is not male and female; for you are all one in Christ Jesus." The other was from Thomas Merton: "We must remember that the Church does not belong to any political power bloc."

When Kobasa's teachers' association refused to back him up, he realized that his days at Kolbe Cathedral High were probably numbered. So he wrote a letter to the head of the diocese, Bishop William Lori. "Your Excellency: It is with both sorrow and dismay that I write you concerning the issues raised below, but I am convinced that it is my obligation to pursue every possible means of resolving this dispute in a spirit of Christian charity rather than confrontation," the letter began.

Kobasa argued that to permanently display the flag in his classroom "would be to act against my conscience as a believing Roman Catholic Christian. My teaching can never take its legitimacy from any symbol except the Cross of Christ. To elevate any national emblem to that level would be for me to ignore the fundamental call of Jesus to compassion without boundaries." He wrote that the threat of dismissal "creates the unmistakable impression that national loyalty is being valued over faithful obedience to the Gospel."

He did not get a response from the bishop. Knowing that he was running out of options, Kobasa decided to take a stand.

At a faculty meeting on October 12, 2005, he asked to speak. " 'This is likely to be my last meeting with this faculty,' " Kobasa remembers saying. "I made it clear that I had never imposed my views on anyone, but that I expected my own conscience to be honored, and since it was not, I would have to take action to preserve it." This was his way of giving "the principal some notice that I was not simply going to resign myself to the policy."

The next morning, October 13, Kobasa did not hesitate.

"I went directly to my classroom and removed the flag and brought it to Mrs. Jakab, and said I could not have it in the same room with the crucifix, which was the image of my faith," he says. "She asked me if I understood the consequence of this. And I assured her I did."

Kobasa was given till the end of the day to leave.

"It was a gift," he says. "I was able to explain to my students what had happened, and why I was making the choice I was, and to tell them what a loss it was for me to not be able to continue with them." Some students "were extremely upset" that day, he says. "I was really stunned by the kinds of testimony I was getting." A few held signs in his defense, including one that said "Save Mr. Kobasa." Quipped Kobasa: "I don't know if it was about salvation in the absolute sense, but I felt very good about it."

Principal Jakab, Superintendent Dames, and Bishop Lori could not be reached for comment. When I called them I was referred each time to Joseph McAleer, spokesman for the Roman Catholic Diocese of Bridgeport. McAleer refused to answer questions but referred me to a statement on the Web site of the diocese.

Here is the entire statement:

> It is with regret that we confirm that Mr. Stephen Kobasa is no longer a member of the faculty of Kolbe Cathedral High School in Bridgeport. It is not our policy to comment on any internal personnel matter. Our Catholic Schools provide a dynamic learning environment in which respect for the opinions of others as well as respect for school property are both key components. The Diocese of Bridgeport has long believed that the American flag is an important fixture in its Catholic School classrooms.

XII

Oh, Those Subversive Artists

1. FBI, Secret Service Take in Art Car Museum—Donna Huanca

Donna Huanca works as a docent at the Art Car Museum, an avant-garde gallery in Houston. Around 10:30 on the morning of November 7, 2001, before she opened the museum, two men wearing suits and carrying leather portfolios came to her door.

"I told them to wait until we opened at eleven," she recalls. "Then they pulled their badges out." The two men were Terrence Donahue of the FBI and Steven Smith of the Secret Service. "They said they had several reports of anti-American activity going on here and wanted to see the exhibit." The museum was running a show called "Secret Wars," which contains many antiwar statements that were commissioned before September 11.

"They just walked in, so I went through with them and gave them a very detailed tour. I asked them if they were familiar with the artists and what the role of art was at a critical time like this," she says. "They were more interested in where the artists were from. They were taking some notes. They were pointing out things that they thought were negative, like a recent painting by Lynn Randolph of the Houston skyline burning, and a devil dancing around, and with George Bush Sr. in the belly of the devil."

There was a surreal moment when they inspected another element of the exhibit. "We had a piece in the middle of the room, a mock surveillance camera pointed to the door of the museum, and they wondered whether they were being recorded," she says.

All in all they were there for about an hour. "As they were leaving they asked me where I went to school, and if my parents knew if I worked at a place like this, and who funded us, and how many people came in to see the exhibit," she says. "I was definitely pale. It was scary, because I was alone, and they were really big guys." Before the agents left the museum Huanca called Tex Kerschen, the curator of the exhibit. "I had just put down a book on COINTELPRO," he says, referring to the FBI's program of infiltrating left-wing groups in the 1960s and early 1970s. "Donna's call confirmed some of my worst suspicions. Donna was frightened, and we're all a little bit shocked that they were going to act against a small art space, to bring to bear that kind of menace, an atmosphere of dread. These old moldy charges of 'anti-American,' 'un-American'—they seem laughable at first, like we can't be accused of anything that silly. But they've started coming down with this."

The director of the Art Car Museum is James Harithas, who served as the director of the Corcoran Gallery of Art in Washington, D.C., in the late 1960s. "It's unbelievable," he says of the visit from the G-men. "People should be worried that their freedoms are being taken away right and left."

Robert Dogium, a spokesman for the FBI in Houston, says the visit was a routine follow-up on a call "from someone who said there was some material or artwork that was of a threatening nature to the president." He says it was no big thing. "While the work there was not

their cup of tea, it was not considered of a threatening nature to anybody or terrorism or anything."

2. Secret Service Goes to Chicago Exhibit—Columbia College Chicago

April 7, 2005, was opening night for a new exhibit at the Glass Cur-
tain Gallery of Columbia College Chicago called "Axis of Evil: The Secret History of Sin."

The exhibit consists of depictions of political postage stamps
about such topics as racism, violence, torture, the Catholic Church,
George W. Bush, John Ashcroft, and the Iraq War. Forty-seven artists,
including some from Canada, England, France, Italy, Japan, Mexico,
Russia, Switzerland, Serbia, and Uruguay, contributed to the traveling
exhibit.

Two Secret Service agents paid a visit just before the doors
opened to the public. They were not art aficionados.

The agents "took photos of some of the works and asked for the
artists' contact information, said CarolAnn Brown, the gallery's director," the AP reported. "Brown said the agents were most interested in
Chicago artist Al Brandtner's work titled *Patriot Act*, which depicted a
sheet of mock 37-cent red, white, and blue stamps showing a revolver
pointed at Bush's head." The day after the opening a Secret Service
agent called the gallery, again seeking contact information for Brandtner, according to the *Daily Southtown*. She did not provide it. Michael
Hernandez de Luna, the curator of the exhibit, told the AP that the
Secret Service inspection "frightens" him. "It starts questioning all
rights, not only my rights or the artists' rights in this room, but questioning the rights of any artist. It seems like we're being watched."

Micki Leventhal, the director of media relations for Columbia College Chicago, backs the exhibit. "We're an art school," she told the

Daily Southtown. "Our position has always been and remains: We support freedom of speech, freedom of artistic expression, and academic freedom."

The Secret Service, meanwhile, defends its inquiry. "In this particular instance, the artwork was brought to our attention by a private citizen in Chicago," says Lorie Lewis, a spokesperson for the Secret Service in Washington. "While the Secret Service certainly respects artistic freedom and people's First Amendment rights of free speech and freedom of expression, we also have a responsibility to look into exhibits and statements when necessary. We've looked at the work, and we've asked questions. We haven't confiscated any artwork or questioned anyone against their wishes. We just need to ensure as best we can that this is nothing more than artwork with a political statement."

3. The Art Professor Prosecuted for His Unusual Supplies—Steve Kurtz

Tragedy and trouble came together for Buffalo art professor Steve Kurtz on May 11, 2004.

That morning, his wife died of a heart attack. When he called 911 and the police showed up, they became suspicious of his artwork, which included petri dishes with transgenic bacteria. Kurtz is a member of the Critical Art Ensemble, which was founded in 1987 to explore "the intersections between art, technology, radical politics, and critical theory," says its Web site, www.critical-art.net. He was preparing to protest biotechnology in a work he was entering for an upcoming exhibition at the Massachusetts Museum of Contemporary Art.

The police called the FBI.

The very next day, even as Kurtz was on his way to the funeral home, the FBI and members of the Joint Terrorism Task Force nabbed him, the Critical Art Ensemble Defense Fund says. "At no point during the 22 hours Kurtz was held and questioned did the agents Mirandize him or inform him he could leave," the group says on its Web site. "Cordoning off half a block around his home, they seized his cat, car, computers, manuscripts, books, equipment, and even his wife's body from the county coroner."

Kurtz "makes art which addresses the politics of biotechnology," explains the Critical Art Ensemble Legal Defense Fund. That art includes "a mobile DNA extraction laboratory for testing food products for possible transgenic contamination. It was this equipment which triggered the Kafkaesque chain of events."

Initially, the U.S. attorney, William Hochul, empaneled a grand jury, presumably to indict Kurtz on bioterrorism charges. But on June 29, 2004, the grand jury refused to do so. Instead, it produced two indictments for mail fraud and wire fraud. The government claims that Kurtz illegally obtained $256 worth of bacteria from Robert Ferrell, former head of the Department of Genetics at the University of Pittsburgh's School of Public Health. Ferrell was also indicted. The indictment says they used "false and fraudulent pretenses and representations" to get the nonlethal bacteria. They face a maximum of twenty years in prison.

"This has everything to do with politics, and nothing to do with crime," Kurtz tells me. "They're charging me with mail fraud because I allegedly broke a material transfer agreement, which at best should be a civil contract dispute, and there isn't one."

Kurtz says he and Ferrell "worked together for five years before the disaster. He's who I always went to to get stuff." Kurtz's supporters say that it's not uncommon for scientists to share their materials.

"The evidence is abundant that neither of these individuals had any criminal intent," said Paul Cambria, Kurtz's attorney, when the indictments came down. "Their intent was simply to educate and enlighten people." Ferrell's attorney, Efrem Grail, said: "Dr. Ferrell is a wonderful academic and an honest man who would never do anything he knew to be wrong."

Kurtz says that if the government can pull this one off, they can make any civil issue into a criminal offense, thus greatly expanding its power. The government is "constructing a climate of fear. They need to show that terrorism is everywhere. It's not just these Islamic guys. Sometimes it's your art teacher."

Plus, he says, "there's the intimidation factor: Activists, scientists, artists, be on call. We're going to come and arrest you."

U.S. Attorney Hochul did not return phone calls for comment on the case.

The prosecution of Kurtz and Ferrell has occasioned protests by artists and civil libertarians in cities around the world, including Amsterdam, London, Paris, and Vienna. The New York Civil Liberties Union and PEN USA have joined the campaign.

Kurtz says he's bearing up surprisingly well.

"It's amazing what you get used to," he says. "The first year was pretty bad. I lost my wife, who was an original member of the Critical Art Ensemble. But I discovered courage I never knew I had. And I just feel very committed to this fight because of the inspiration of people who have rallied to my case."

4. Artist Beams Bush Monkeys *After Being Booted from Gallery—*
Christopher Savido

Christopher Savido made a portrait of President Bush out of tiny images of chimpanzees. The piece, entitled *Bush Monkeys,* was to be part of an exhibition called "Animal's Paradise" at the Chelsea Market in Manhattan.

The exhibition, slated to last a month, opened on December 9,

2004. But it didn't last the weekend. A manager at the market "saw the piece, and the guy just kind of flipped out," Bucky Turco, organizer of the exhibit, told Reuters. According to Turco, the manager said, "The show is over. Get this work down, or I'm going to arrest you."

Savido told AP that this was "a blatant act of censorship."

Animal Magazine, which had organized the show, wanted people to see Savido's work. So it raised money from anonymous donors, and on December 21 it began posting the image on the Jumbotron on the Manhattan-side entrance of the Holland Tunnel.

According to the magazine's Web site (www.animalnewyork.com) that image was broadcast "approximately ten times an hour for a month," reaching four hundred thousand drivers a day. On top of that, Savido auctioned his work on eBay. "After the first morning of bidding, the controversial 'Bush Monkeys' painting secured a high bid of $13,000, almost four times the list price that was put on the painting in the *Animal Magazine* art show from which it was banned," the Web site says.

Animal Magazine and Savido said they were donating the proceeds of the auction to two efforts. The first is called "Art for Armor," which "helps soldiers' parents to supply their children with effective body armor," says the Web site. The second is "Art for Education," which "provides scholarships for disadvantaged urban youth who wish to pursue a career in the arts."

5. Flag-in-Toilet Art Creates a Stink—Stephen Pearcy

An art exhibit in the cafeteria of the California Department of Justice was causing quite a stir in the summer of 2005. Actually, one particular piece of art: a depiction of a map of the United States draped in a flag and going down a toilet.

The artist is California lawyer Stephen Pearcy, and his work was part of an exhibit of "more than 30 works by lawyer artists and pieces with overt legal themes," the *San Francisco Chronicle* reported. "The sponsor of the show is California Lawyers for the Arts, a nonprofit group founded in the Bay Area in 1974 to aid artists with their legal issues."

The California Republican Party demanded the removal of the artwork, right-wing bloggers called Pearcy a traitor, and one blog even suggested he should be killed.

In a statement accompanying his flag-in-toilet piece Pearcy explained his motivations: "I painted this on the 4th of July, 2003, to show what direction this country was (and still is) headed under the Bush Administration. It also confronted the absurd display of 'fanatical patriotism' following 9/11.

"This country is going down the toilet," his statement continues, citing the unjust occupation of Iraq, the torture of detainees, conservative domination of the media, the lack of corporate accountability, and censorship, among other items. "We'll remain in the toilet until we vote out the party whose goal is to limit our freedom."

"I don't know why we need to tolerate the cheap artwork of a gadfly with a worldview that is so offensive to a majority of the people," said Karen Hanretty, a spokeswoman for the California Republican Party. She added that Pearcy's painting is "so blatantly offensive to our military and what we are doing in Iraq to fight a war on terrorism." Hanretty demanded that attorney general Bill Lockyer take Pearcy's painting down.

Lockyer's director of communications, Nathan Barankin, said the AG wouldn't consider it. "Expressing your political views is not a crime, at least not yet, until Karen Hanretty has her way," Barankin told KXTV.

But it may endanger you.

A right-wing blog, caosblog.com, solicited ideas for harming Pearcy. "I'm taking submissions for a contest about the anti-American left," wrote Cao, the nom de plume of the woman who runs the blog. "I'm looking for a visual representation of what you would do if you were George Washington and someone like Stephen Pearcy was in your command. George Washington shot and hung 'dissenters.' "

She provided a visual representation of her own on the site, displaying a photo of Pearcy with a blindfold superimposed over his eyes. Less than an inch from his forehead was a gun held by a masked soldier. Next to Pearcy's torso were the words "Traitor" and "Infidel." Cao did not respond to e-mails for comment. Pearcy told me the site clearly suggests "I should be executed. It's intended to make me fear for my safety because of my political expression."

And he did fear for his safety.

"Bottom line, I'm concerned somebody might feel they would be heroic if they carry out what she seems to be indicating," he said, adding that his wife, Virginia, was also very concerned. Some people who disagreed with Pearcy countered his message with a nonviolent one of their own. A group called Move America Forward hosted an "I Love America" art exhibit and rally on July 28 in downtown Sacramento outside of the building where Pearcy's "anti-American" piece was being exhibited, the group says in a press release. "The offensive material displayed at the Department of Justice building sends the message to the terrorists around the world that American morale is low," said Melanie Morgan, chair of Move America Forward.

On August 21, the California attorney general's office took Pearcy's piece down, nine days before the exhibit closed. The decision was "out of concern for the events going on in the Middle East right now," spokesman Barankin told the *Sacramento Bee*. When I spoke with Barankin he told me that he didn't consider this to be caving in to pressure from right-wing groups because the painting was taken to Lockyer's office.

For his part Pearcy would have preferred that his painting remained in the art exhibit for the duration. And he doesn't buy Barankin's rationale. "Thus far, I have been unable to establish a direct connection between the content of my painting and Middle East events," he says. But he was flattered, in a way, with where it ended up.

Says Pearcy: "It was moved into the AG's own personal office, where it ironically sat directly across from another painting that said, 'Censorship is Un-American.' I must admit that might be the most honorable way that I can imagine having my art censored from public view."

XIII

His Royal Highness Is Coming to Town

1. A Nonviolent Protester Convicted Under Assassination Statute—
Brett A. Bursey

On October 24, 2002, Brett A. Bursey went to the airport in Columbia, South Carolina, to protest a visit by President Bush. Bursey, the director of the South Carolina Progressive Network, was on public property holding a sign that said "No More War for Oil." Bush was there to campaign for Lindsey Graham.

"This was a public rally," says Bursey, "and there were like five thousand people there, with buttons and signs for Graham." But it was Bursey and his sign that drew the attention of law enforcement.

They ordered him to go to a so-called free-speech zone a half mile away. Bursey said he already was in a free-speech zone: the United States of America. But he offered to move one hundred yards away.

That wasn't enough.

The police told him that if he didn't move he'd be arrested.

Bursey didn't move.

They proceeded to arrest him. Here's the conversation, as he recalls it:

"Sir, what are you arresting me for?"

"Trespassing."

"Is it because of the content of my sign?"

"Yes."

Bursey, who has been an activist in South Carolina since the 1960s, had already successfully litigated a case that made it clear you could not be convicted of trespassing on public property. So he says he felt confident that he'd be cleared.

"I said, 'Put the cuffs on me. You do what you got to do; I do what I got to do.' "

After he was arrested, the state eventually did drop the charges.

But then, a couple of days later, the U.S. attorney indicted him for violating a statute having to do with presidential assassinations, kidnappings, and threats.

The U.S. attorney was Strom Thurmond Jr., son of the segregationist senator.

"I was stunned," says Bursey, who says this is the first time a protester had been slapped with this charge. Thurmond's prosecution of Bursey drew the attention of members of Congress. On May 27, 2003, Representative Barney Frank, Democrat of Massachusetts, sent a letter, signed by ten other House members, to Attorney General John Ashcroft, saying that Ashcroft's persecution of Bursey "is in fact a threat to the freedom of expression we should all be defending." The letter continues:

> There is no plausible argument that can be made that Mr. Bursey was threatening the President by holding a sign which the President found politically offensive. . . . Being politically annoying to the President of the United States is not a criminal offense. This prosecution smacks of the use of the Sedition Acts 200 years ago to protect the President from political discomfort. It was wrong then, and it is wrong now.

But Strom Thurmond Jr. did not drop the prosecution. In fact, he prevailed.

On January 6, 2004, U.S. Magistrate Bristow Marchant "acknowledged Bursey was not a threat to Bush during the President's visit to Columbia," the *State* newspaper reported. "But the judge dismissed Bursey's free speech defense and ruled the protester had no right to be as close to Bush as Bursey wanted."

Bursey was fined $500. At his sentencing Bursey said, "The fight for free speech and the rule of law does not end with this ruling. It must intensify, or we will soon not recognize our own country." So Bursey appealed. "Bush is like Catherine the Great, who would use the Russian Imperial Guard to clear the rabble off the streets," he says.

And though Chief Judge Diana Gribbon Motz of the Court of Appeals for the Fourth Circuit called it "an uncommonly silly prosecution by the government," that court upheld Bursey's conviction on October 21, 2005.

The U.S. Supreme Court, on January 17, 2006, declined to hear Bursey's appeal. His conviction stands.

2. Protester Reluctantly Takes Plea—Thomas C. Frazier

Thomas C. Frazier works as an investigator in the prosecutor's office of California's South Coast Air Quality Management District, the antipollution agency in the Orange County area.

On October 16, 2003, he decided to take the day off to go to San Bernardino from his home in Santa Ana. His purpose, he says, was "to engage in a legal and peaceful protest" against George W. Bush. The president was in town that day at the Radisson Hotel and Convention Center to support the candidacy of Arnold Schwarzenegger.

Frazier called the Radisson to get directions, and he drove over and parked where they told him to. He then reached into the trunk of his 1987 Volkswagen Jetta and took out his homemade sign. It had two cardboard posterboards attached to a wooden base. One side said, "Shock & Awe" = "Maim & Murder" and the other said, "Indict Bush—Crimes Against Humanity." He also took with him some bumper stickers that said, "Stop the Madness."

Walking out of the parking lot "I was confronted by a charging police officer (later identified as John Montecino)," Frazier wrote in a complaint he filed with the San Bernardino Police Department. "For no apparent reason, Officer Montecino raced towards me screaming, 'No, no, no, no. Get there, Get there!' . . . Without any provocation, Officer Montecino then grabbed my sign by enveloping my arms and sign together in one rapid swoop."

"Can't I just get across the street to show my protest?" Frazier asked, according to his complaint.

"Officer Montecino responded, 'Give me the sign,' and snatched the sign away from me while still encasing my arms," Frazier wrote.

"I then asked Officer Montecino, 'Can I have my sign back, and I'll just leave then?' Officer Montecino responded by stating, 'I don't have time for this,' while simultaneously striking my right forearm with a smashing blow with one side of a set of handcuffs. . . . I asked him, 'Sir, why am I being arrested?' and he replied, 'For not doing what I told you to do.' " Another officer took Frazier down to the police station, and Montecino arrived a little later. "You're being arrested for obstructing a police officer. Your sign could have been a weapon," Montecino said, according to Frazier's complaint.

The police report says, "During a Presidential visit, the listed defendant entered a restricted area and did not comply with officer's request and demands. He was arrested for obstructing and delaying an officer."

Frazier filed his formal complaint against Montecino for "erroneously and unlawfully arresting me, [for] physically and verbally abusing me, [for] illegally confiscating my personal property, [and for] violating my civil rights of freedom to assemble and freedom of speech."

I called Montecino to get his side of the story. "I can't discuss it," he told me.

Meanwhile, Frazier still faced the charge of obstructing an officer. If convicted, he faced a $1,000 fine and up to six months in jail.

Frazier says the DA in San Bernardino offered him a deal. "He said I could plead down to a misdemeanor disturbing-the-peace charge, and it would be like getting a jaywalking ticket," says Frazier.

This was a tough one for Frazier. "I went back and forth," he says. He wanted to fight it, but "San Bernardino is a pretty conservative area, so I would have been taking a gamble there."

Frazier pleaded to the misdemeanor.

3. "FUGW"—Frank Van Den Bosch

When Frank Van Den Bosch heard that George Bush was coming through Platteville, Wisconsin, on May 7, 2004, he knew he wanted to be there to protest.

Van Den Bosch lives only thirty miles to the north, and he and his wife had helped set up a group called Students for Peace and Justice when she was at the University of Wisconsin–Platteville, he says. Van Den Bosch considered what to write on his poster. "I couldn't think of any one particular issue I wanted to address, and I was so completely saddened and angered by what was happening that the most concise statement I could come up with was 'FUGW.' "

When Van Den Bosch arrived at the protest he joined a group of about twenty others. But soon his sign drew attention. "An officer came over and said, 'You can't display your sign,' " Van Den Bosch recalls. "She said she had checked with the Secret Service, and they didn't like the sign.

"And I said, 'Well, that's their problem.' "

But Van Den Bosch did agree to modify the sign. Under the F, he wrote in smaller letters "ree" to spell "Free," and, under the U, he wrote "s" to spell "Us." "But they weren't satisfied with that," he says. "A sergeant came over and tried to take the sign away from me, but I rolled it up and stood in the back a bit." When Van Den Bosch saw the Bush-Cheney buses coming he wanted to display his sign again.

"I unrolled my sign and stood there," says Van Den Bosch, "and then they came over and grabbed the sign and said, 'We told you you couldn't show that sign.' They walked me over in front of a frat house where a bunch of guys had been harassing us, and they handcuffed me there to the cheering of the guys. Then they put me in an unmarked car and drove me into town, fingerprinted me and photographed me, and gave me a ticket for disorderly conduct."

Lieutenant Tom Schmid of the Platteville Police Department gives a slightly different account of what happened. "We had a person complain about the sign, and we went down and asked the gentleman not to show the sign, because there were kids in the area and it didn't seem appropriate," Schmid says. "Later on, he showed the sign again, and we went down and arrested him and charged him with disorderly conduct."

Why does holding such a sign constitute disorderly conduct?

"It seemed to annoy and disturb others," says Schmid, "and when you have conduct that tends to annoy or disturb others, that's disorderly conduct."

Sergeant Michelle Hechel, who spoke with Van Den Bosch at the protest, denies that she mentioned the Secret Service or that the Secret Service had anything to do with the incident. "He had a sign," she says. "It was offensive. And we asked him to not show it."

As to whether he has the right to display an offensive sign, Hechel says, "Once it starts offending other people, which it did in that area, he was asked to not display that. It was not appropriate. We said he could use a different sign, but he chose not to."

Van Den Bosch says his arrest shows "the fangs and teeth of the state. The chilling part is, they knew they were violating my civil rights. Any eighth-grade civics class will teach you that you have the right to express yourself."

The case against Van Den Bosch was dismissed on May 27, 2004. Van Den Bosch filed a civil complaint against the city, which settled with him in August of 2004. "The city came with an offer of $6,500, plus my attorney fees, and my lawyer recommended that I take it," he says. "The total came to $12,086.45. It's about as much justice as we can get, but it's not really justice."

4. Arrested for "Love America, Hate Bush" Sign, Protesters Sue—Nicole and Jeff Rank

Nicole and Jeff Rank were in Charleston, West Virginia, on July 4, 2004, to protest a visit by President Bush to the state capitol.

The Ranks, who are from Corpus Christi, Texas, gathered outside the capitol. People near them "wore pro-Bush T-shirts and Bush-Cheney campaign buttons, some of which were sold on the capitol grounds," according to the *Charleston Gazette*. Not the Ranks. They were wearing T-shirts that read "Love America, Hate Bush," the *Gazette* reported.

The police evidently did not take kindly to that.

"Law enforcement officers told the couple to take the shirts off, cover them, or get out," AP reported. "When they refused and sat down, they were arrested." The Charleston police alleged that they were in "a no-trespassing zone and refused to leave," the *Gazette* said. The two were charged with trespassing, but a judge dismissed the charges on July 15.

Andrew Schneider, executive director of the ACLU of West Virginia, which helped defend the couple, called their arrest a "glaring violation of the First Amendment," according to the *Gazette*.

"We'll continue to exercise our right to free expression when we see fit," Jeff Rank told AP, adding, "We're not professional protesters. We're going to get on with our lives." But that was difficult, since Nicole Rank was temporarily suspended from her job as a deputy environmental liaison officer for FEMA.

On July 19, 2004, the Charleston City Council ate crow. "The city does hereby apologize to Nicole and Jeff Rank," it said in a resolution, AP reported. The resolution also stated: "If Nicole and Jeff Rank did nothing other than peaceably exercise their right of free speech and expression as guaranteed by our constitutions, they should not have been arrested or charged with a crime."

On September 14, 2004, the ACLU filed suit against the Secret Service and a White House advance man on behalf of the Ranks. "This is a simple case," says ACLU senior staff attorney Chris Hansen. "Two Americans went to see their president and to express their disagreement with his policies respectfully and peacefully. They were arrested at the direction of federal officials. That is precisely what the First Amendment was adopted to prevent."

5. Police Close Down Abu Ghraib Street Theater Before Bush Arrives—
Lancaster, Pennsylvania

When some antiwar activists from Lancaster, Pennsylvania, heard that President Bush and his motorcade would be coming through nearby Smoketown on the afternoon of July 9, 2004, they decided to plan an unusual protest.

Rather than carrying the usual signs, they opted for street theater of a novel kind. They decided to replicate the human pyramid at Abu Ghraib: the stacking of naked Iraqi prisoners. "We thought it would be an effective way to show our revulsion about the war," said Tristan Egolf a few weeks later. "We took a specific photo of the Abu Ghraib scandal, and we planned to arrange ourselves exactly as in the photo."

Egolf and seven others waited for the Bush motorcade by the side of Old Philadelphia Pike. There were many more Bush supporters there than protesters, he said.

Shortly before 3:00 P.M., Egolf's group heard cheers. Thinking that the motorcade was approaching, the men stripped down to their thongs and got in position. A woman with the group pretended to be a U.S. soldier mocking the faux prisoners.

The reaction from the Bush supporters was immediate, said Egolf. "They called us scumbags and faggots," he said. "One guy came up to us and said, 'I don't care how many people we have to kill as long as my gasoline prices are lower.' "

After a couple of minutes "the police came in and started pulling us apart," Egolf said. They handcuffed six of the seven men without reading them their rights or charging them with anything, according to Egolf and three of the others. "They took us down a bank and out of view of the crowd and put us down in a ditch," Egolf said. They stayed there until the Bush motorcade was well out of town, and then the police took them down to the East Lampeter Township station. There they were given tickets for disorderly conduct and released after about three hours.

Ben Keely was one of those arrested. "I was roughed up a little bit," he said, explaining that the handcuffs were too tight on him. "My left hand was numb for about three days afterwards." Keely views street theater as an important way to get a message out. "Holding signs doesn't always get the point across," he said. "We want to make people aware of what's going on in the world around us."

The police evidently were looking to pin an obscenity or indecent exposure charge on the protesters. "I heard one of the state cops going up and down the line asking pro-Bush people if they had photos that would show the protesters' genitalia, because it 'would be easier to charge them,'" recalls Van Gosse, a professor at Franklin and Marshall College and a member of the Lancaster Peace and Justice Coalition.

The protesters believe their civil liberties were trampled on. "It's a pretty clear-cut Bill of Rights violation," Egolf said. The Pennsylvania chapter of the ACLU agrees.

"Street theater is a constitutionally protected form of expression," says Vic Walczak, litigation director of the ACLU of Pennsylvania, which assisted the protesters. "As long as they're not blocking traffic they have every right to engage in this venerable and creative form of protest."

Lieutenant Jim Ely of the East Lampeter Township police department says, "I'm sorry, we're not going to comment."

All six of the protesters pleaded not guilty on July 19.

On October 15, the district attorney dropped all charges.

DA Donald Totaro said the protesters' actions were protected under the First Amendment. Prosecutors, he said, "must follow and uphold the laws of Pennsylvania and of this nation."

6. Anti-Cheney Protester Arrested, Cleared, Wins Victory—John Blair

On February 8, 2002, Vice President Dick Cheney was visiting Evansville, Indiana, to campaign for Representative John Hostettler.

One lone protester, John Blair, was walking on a public sidewalk and was carrying a sign that read: "Cheney: 19th Century Energy Man."

For this, he was arrested.

"I was arrested for nothing more than exercising my rights as a citizen in what I thought was a free country," Blair wrote in an article for *Counterpunch*, which broke the story. Blair was standing outside Evansville's government center, across the street from the convention center where Cheney and Hostettler were gathering for a fund-raiser.

"The main cop informed me that if I did not go more than a block away to the area he apparently had just arbitrarily decided was to be used by protesters that I would be arrested," Blair wrote. "I complied and started to walk away. When I turned to ask if it was OK to go to the parking lot where hundreds of people were either leaving work or arriving to attend the event, he instructed his uniformed men to arrest me."

Blair was at first charged with disorderly conduct. Then the prosecutor increased the charge to a Class A misdemeanor of resisting law enforcement. "Now I am facing what could be a year in jail for my political crime of carrying a sign to a political event," Blair wrote in *Counterpunch*.

But the case against Blair was dropped. "I dismissed this case yesterday. I didn't think the evidence established a case that would be successful in court," Stan Levco, the prosecuting attorney for Vanderburgh County, Indiana, told me on February 20, 2002. "I don't think they were wrong to arrest him under the circumstances. They thought it was a safety issue, and I wouldn't second-guess them."

"They shouldn't even have approached me in the first place," Blair responds. "Carrying a sign isn't an illegal act in America. At least it wasn't before Bush-Cheney. I'm a little disappointed that Stan thinks there was a safety issue involved, but clearly he understands that I was within my rights." Blair runs a local environmental group called Valley Watch. Before becoming an activist he was a photographer for UPI. In fact, he won the Pulitzer Prize for news photography back in 1979.

He takes his civil liberties seriously. "I have a bumper sticker on my car that says, 'Talk is cheap. Free speech isn't,' " he says. "I have a pretty good understanding of what my rights are. I know when to bitch, and when to walk away. I wasn't beaten or dragged, but I had my civil liberties just ripped away from me."

In January 2003, Blair and the ACLU of Indiana sued the city of Evansville for violating his constitutional rights.

On March 18, 2005, District Judge Larry McKinney ruled in favor of Blair.

> The restriction of protesters to an area 500 feet away from the only entrance used by attendees, and on the opposite end of the building from where Vice President Cheney would enter the facility and from where the majority of people attending the event would park, burdened speech substantially more than was necessary to further the Defendants' goals of safety. This limitation significantly curtailed Blair's ability to convey his message.

The judge ruled that the city had violated his First Amendment rights, as well as his Fourth Amendment rights for arresting him without probable cause. Evansville city attorney David Jones blamed the Secret Service.

"Jones said the Secret Service refused to provide evidence, testimony, and witnesses he needed to make the city's case," the *Evansville Courier & Press* reported.

Said Jones: "We've been used like a pair of work gloves, and when we were no longer handy, we were just discarded."

For his part, Blair was happy with the ruling. "I got a decent financial settlement out of it that paid my attorneys, and also decent remuneration for my time in jail," he says. "It was just an excellent decision that really spanked the police and the Secret Service for putting me in that position."

7. The Crawford Five Prevail

On May 3, 2003, demonstrators were trying to go down to Bush's ranch outside of Crawford, Texas, to protest the Iraq War. As the group tried to move through Crawford the police set up a barricade and blocked them from proceeding.

"Our intention was not to be in the city limits of Crawford," says Amanda Jack, who lives in Austin and was acting as a legal observer on May 3 to make sure no one's rights were violated. "We wanted to get as close as possible to the ranch," which is farther down the road. Jack was in the last car of the caravan, and she saw the other cars pulled over. Some of the occupants had gotten out with their signs to see what was going on, she says. But they were not demonstrating there.

Police Chief Donnie Tidmore ordered everyone to get back in their cars within three minutes or face arrest, Jack says. "I went back up to ask Chief Tidmore if people could have more time, and as I was doing this, deputies came up and started to arrest one of our members. Another legal observer was trying to find out the name of the person arrested when she, too, got arrested. I asked, where are you taking these people? And they arrested me."

Jack, the assistant director of Casa Marianella, a shelter for recently arrived immigrants and refugees, was held overnight in the nearby Waco jail with the four others: Ken Zarifis, Amara Maliszewski, Trish Major, and Michael Machicek. The group became known as the Crawford Five.

Zarifis was an eighth-grade English teacher in Austin. He, too, was a legal observer on May 3. "My intention was just to keep an eye on what was going on, and if civil liberties were being violated, I would jot them down," he says.

But like Amanda Jack's, his watchfulness was not appreciated. Zarifis saw the police arresting two people, including another legal observer, so he went up to the policeman. "I asked the officer what his name and badge number was, and he told me, 'Step off the road, I'm going to arrest you.' I wasn't really in the road, but I stepped back four or five feet off the grass, and I said, 'I still need to ask why you're arresting them,' and he then arrested me and took me to the van."

Trish Major was the communications director at the Dallas Peace Center. She had come to Crawford with her fourteen-year-old daughter and her daughter's friend "to see the Peace House" there, she says. She had gotten wind that protesters were coming, so she went looking for them. She saw the cars come and pull over and the people pile out with their signs. She heard Chief Tidmore tell people to get back in their cars, and she says he heard him warn, "If you leave your protest signs, you'll be cited for littering." Major did not have a car nearby, so she picked up a sign and went off to the side of the road.

"A television reporter came up to me and started asking me questions," she says. "I started answering her questions. In the middle of that I saw five or six law enforcement officers coming toward me. And they said, 'Put down your sign,' and I was kind of wondering whether I should do this, and would I be cited for littering. They put my hands behind my back and handcuffed me." It was the first time she had ever been arrested.

Michael Machicek had a similar experience. He came to the area on a bus with members of the Dallas Peace Center, and he had supper at the Crawford Peace House. Afterward he saw the caravan come through, and he was curious.

"I wanted to see what was going on," he says, "so I took off walking toward the highway. I was standing by the side of the road when I was hailed by a policeman, who turned out to be Police Chief Tidmore. He said, 'You, get over there with the rest of them, get in your car, and get out of here.' I wasn't with the rest of them, and I didn't have a car. I wasn't able to do what he ordered, and I needed to explain to him what my situation was. I told him I walked from the Crawford Peace House, and I asked him if he could give me a ride back. He said, 'We'll give you a ride. We'll give you a ride to the jail.' " Machicek says a deputy then came over, "threw me on the hood of the car, handcuffed me, and marched me to the van."

At trial their lawyer, Jim Harrington, director of the Texas Civil Rights Project, cross-examined Tidmore and extracted an alarming—and telling—concession from him. Harrington asked him about the city's ordinance that required demonstrators to apply for a permit fifteen days in advance. Harrington asked "whether one of the defendants would have violated the ordinance by sporting political buttons, such as those that read 'No Nukes' and 'Peace,' without the permit," according to the *Waco Tribune-Herald*.

"It could be a sign of demonstration," Tidmore responded, according to the paper.

Still, it took a local jury only ninety minutes on February 16, 2004, to convict the five peace activists of violating the municipal parade and procession ordinance. They were fined between $200 and $500 each.

The Crawford Five appealed—and won.

On July 9, 2004, McLennan County judge Tom Ragland said the ordinance was "overly broad on its face," and he added that "the manner in which it was implemented and enforced by the City of Crawford contravened the First Amendment." Then the Crawford Five and the Texas Civil Rights Project filed a federal civil rights suit against the city of Crawford, Tidmore, the sheriff and the sheriff's chief deputy, and the Texas Department of Public Safety.

On May 27, 2005, the parties reached a settlement, with the defendants agreeing to pay $43,000 to the Crawford Five and the Texas Civil Rights Project. Harrington said the case represents an "enormously important victory." The ordinance, he said in a statement, was "a shameless attempt to ban any adverse political protest near President Bush's ranch." It gave "unfettered discretion to the police chief to decide who can and cannot protest and impermissibly discriminated on the basis of the content of the speech. . . . This is un-American, anti-democratic, and unconstitutional."

8. Criticizing Cheney to His Face Is Assault?—Steve Howards

Steve Howards says he used to fantasize about what he'd say to President Bush or Vice President Cheney if he ever got the chance.

That opportunity arrived on June 16, 2006, the same day he says he read about U.S. fatalities in Iraq reaching 2,500.

Howards says he was taking two of his kids to their Suzuki piano camp in Beaver Creek, Colorado. They were walking across the outdoor public mall area when all of a sudden he saw Cheney there.

"I didn't even know he was in town," Howards says. "He was walking through the area shaking hands. Initially, I walked past him. Then I said to myself, 'I can't in good conscience let this opportunity pass by.' So I approached him, I got about two feet away, and I said in a very calm tone of voice. 'Your policies in Iraq are reprehensible.' And then I walked away."

Howards says he knew the administration has a "history of making problems" for people who protest its policies, so he wanted to leave off at that. But the Secret Service did not take kindly to his comment. "About ten minutes later I came back through the mall with my eight-year-old son in tow," Howards recalls, "and this Secret Service man came out of the shadows, and his exact words were, 'Did you assault the vice president?' "

Here's how Howards says he responded: "No, but I did tell Mr. Cheney the way I felt about the war in Iraq, and if Mr. Cheney wants to be shielded from public criticism, he should avoid public places. If exercising my constitutional rights to free speech is against the law, then you should arrest me."

Which is just what the agent, Virgil D. "Gus" Reichle Jr., proceeded to do. "He grabbed me and cuffed my hands behind my back in the presence of my eight-year-old son, and told me I was being charged with assault of the vice president," Howards recalls. He says he told the agent, "I can't abandon my eight-year-old son in a public mall."

According to Howards Reichle responded: "We'll call social services." Before that could happen, however, "my son ran away and found my wife," who was nearby, Howards says.

"First of all, I was scared," Howards recalls. "They wouldn't tell my wife where they were taking me. Second of all, I was incredulous this could be happening in the United States of America. This is what I read about happening in Tiananmen Square. They hauled me away to Eagle County jail and kept me with my hands cuffed behind my back for three hours."

At the jail, the charge against him was reduced to harassment, he says, and he was released on $500 bond. The Eagle County DA's office eventually dropped that charge. On October 3, Howards sued Reichle for depriving him of his First Amendment right of free speech and his Fourth Amendment right to be protected from illegal seizure. Howards and his attorney, David Lane, have not demanded a specific dollar amount. "We will go to trial and let a Colorado jury decide what type of damages are appropriate," says Howards. "This isn't about anything I did. This is about what I said. There is a frontal assault occurring on our constitutional right to free speech. We brought this suit because of our belief that this administration's attempt to suppress free speech is a greater threat to the long-term integrity of this nation than ten Osama bin Ladens."

Reichle did not return my call for comment. Nor did he respond to the *New York Times* for its article on this incident.

Lon Garner, special agent in charge at the Secret Service's Denver office, says he has "no reaction" to the lawsuit. "It's in litigation," he says. "We have no comment."

Before his encounter with Cheney, Howards says he had a clean record. "I was never arrested before," he says. "I don't have so much as a speeding ticket."

XIV

This Campaign Event Is Closed

1. Denied Entrance in Dubuque—Bill Ward, Nick Lucy, and Jan Oswald

On May 7, 2004, George W. Bush went to Dubuque to campaign at the convention center. It was billed as a public event, but it was anything but.

Only self-proclaimed Bush supporters could get in. Republican organizers excluded even Bill Ward, World War II vet (45th Infantry Division) and a former commander of the local American Legion chapter. Ward had gone to pick up tickets a few days ahead of time.

Here is his account: "When I got up there they asked to see my license and so forth, and I showed it to them. And then this young guy asked, 'Are you a Bush backer?'

"And I said, 'No, I didn't vote for him the first time, and I'm not going to vote for him this time.'

"And he said, 'Get out.'

"I said, 'I don't have to take this crap. I'm a World War II vet.'

"He said, 'Escort him out.'

"I said, 'I don't need an escort. I can find my way out.'

Ward proceeded right down to the offices of the *Dubuque Telegraph Herald.* "I was teed off," he says.

Nick Lucy is a Vietnam veteran and a past commander of the American Legion in Dubuque. "I blow 'Taps' two or three times a week for veterans," he says. But his service and his patriotism were not enough to get him into the Bush event either.

"One of my Republican friends, a prominent businessman, gave me two tickets," he recalls. "I promised to go because I've seen almost every president since Johnson."

But once he got to the checkpoint the security staff said, "Your name is not on the list."

Lucy explained who had given him the tickets, and he suggested that the security staff call up his Republican friend then and there. "I don't care who you want me to call," one of the security people said.

When Lucy tried to take the man's picture "he put his notebook in front of his face," Lucy says. And then the man told the police to get him out of there.

"If we can't listen to one another, that's not going to make America better," he says.

Four members of Women in Black, a feminist peace group, were also denied entrance, even though they had proper tickets. Jan Oswald was one of them. "I went the morning they were giving out tickets," she says. "It was a two-and-a-half-hour wait in the Dubuque Building, which is downtown."

The screening process was obvious, she recalls. "Everyone was being asked whether they supported the president, or were they registered Republicans, or would they put up a sign in their yard or a sticker in their car." But for some reason, when she got to the front of the line, the woman handing out tickets let her buy four of them without any questions asked, except for the names and phone numbers of all four women, Oswald says.

On May 7, since she had a ticket, she expected to get into the event. "We walked up to the check people, and we had our driver's licenses out and the tickets, so they looked up our names and they said we were on the list to get in. But then a gentleman said, 'You do not look like the kind of people who are here for the right reasons.' " "I responded, 'You know, I'm an American. I've got a ticket that matches. I have identification, and I want to see the president.'

"The man said, 'This is a private affair. You are not welcome.' At that point, he ripped up our tickets."

Her response to that?

"We told him it didn't seem like the kind of America we wanted to live in, and we walked away," she says.

Steve Bateman, chair of the Dubuque County Republican Party, says this screening policy was not his idea. "I wasn't in charge of President Bush coming to Dubuque," he says. "The Bush campaign ran the event."

The Bush campaign did not return phone calls for comment.

2. County Supervisor Yanked for Hidden Kerry Shirt— Jayson Nelson

President Bush came to Wisconsin on July 14, 2004, and gave a speech in a town called Ashwaubenon, and Jayson Nelson wanted to hear him.

Nelson is an elected official. As an Outagamie County supervisor, he says he was notified that there were extra tickets for the event if he wanted one. He did, and after giving his ID and Social Security number he received a VIP pass a few days before Bush came to town. On the morning of Bush's visit Nelson, a Democrat, attended a Kerry rally and was wearing a "Kerry for President" T-shirt. Then, when he went to the Bush rally, he buttoned up a blue denim shirt over the Kerry one.

As he approached the final screening point Nelson says a Republican event staffer demanded that he step out of the line and take off his top shirt.

"At first, I thought she wasn't even talking to me," he recalls, "because who tells you that stuff? So I ignored her and kept going forward, and then she told me again, 'You, you, you, step out of line. You've got to take off your shirt.' "

When he did so, the screener pounced.

"She must have thought I was bin Laden or something because her eyes got big, and she lunged at me and grabbed the ticket and tore it up," he says. "Then she called the Ashwaubenon Police Department on me, and they came over and said, 'What's the problem here? Do you have a ticket?' And I said, 'I had one but they just took it!' "

She told the police to look at his T-shirt, and the police told him he couldn't be there and to get going. "It was apparent to me that if I was going to debate it, I was going to get arrested," he says.

On his way out, the Secret Service also stopped him. "They took my driver's license and wrote down my Social Security number and telephone number," he says. "I started to ask, 'What's going on here? Is a T-shirt illegal?' And they said, 'No, we do this for all of the events, even Kerry's.' "

The Bush-Cheney campaign did not return a phone call for comment. But Merrill Smith, the Midwestern regional spokeswoman for the Bush-Cheney campaign, did talk to the Associated Press, which broke this story. "These events are for people who are going to get out and support the President and who are going to work on his behalf between now and November 2," Smith told AP, though she said she wasn't familiar with the particular incident.

The Ashwaubenon police minimize their involvement. "There was no report on that and no arrest made," says Margene Roshak of the police department. "The Secret Service asked him to leave and escorted him out."

For his part, Nelson is still angry about this. "I was almost treated like a criminal," he says. He finds it ironic that he was excluded from the Resch Center, where Bush was speaking. "I was a foreman and superintendent in building that building," he says. "To get kicked out of it just because I had a T-shirt on—I don't see it. No one asked who I was voting for when I built it."

3. No Antiwar Signs Allowed at Democratic Convention— Medea Benjamin and Vincent Lavery

John Kerry, in his acceptance speech at the 2004 Democratic convention in Boston, made an inspiring call to defend free speech. "We are here to affirm that when Americans stand up and speak their minds and say America can do better, that is not a challenge to patriotism; it is the heart and soul of patriotism."

But on the floor of his own convention, when two Americans— one a delegate and one with a press pass—tried to stand up and speak their minds, and to say that America can do better, they were not allowed to do so.

Medea Benjamin had a press pass for the Democratic convention. She is a co-founder of Global Exchange, a group devoted to human rights and economic and social justice, and she is also a co-founder of CodePink, a feminist peace group. "I went onto the floor of the convention on Tuesday night when Teresa Heinz was speaking and opened up a banner that said, 'End the Occupation of Iraq.' It was maybe three feet by two feet. Pink, of course," she recalls. "I was immediately surrounded by police, who tried to take it away from me. They said, 'Only official signs are allowed.' And then I heard Teresa Heinz say, 'The true patriot is one who speaks truth to power,' so I started speaking truth to power, and I started yelling, 'Will John Kerry bring the troops home? Will John Kerry take an antiwar stand?' Then I got lifted in the air, and as they were dragging me out, I was yelling, 'End the occupation, bring the troops home.' "

Benjamin says she was held for about half an hour, and was questioned not only by the DNC's own security staff but also by the Boston police and the Secret Service. "They questioned me on everything from my Social Security number and birthday and marital status to my political persuasion," she says.

Vincent Lavery last went to a Democratic convention in 1968, as a Robert Kennedy delegate. He was a delegate again this time, for John Edwards. Lavery is also one of the co-founders of Peace Fresno. I spoke by phone with Lavery on the Sunday morning after the convention. He was back in California, working at the Kerry/Edwards Fresno County campaign, which he co-chairs. He was about to go speak to a Kerry rally with the United Farm Workers, but he was still burning about the treatment he received on the floor of the convention.

"A letter came from the DNC a week or ten days before, listing about twenty things we shouldn't and couldn't do, and one was no signs," he recalls. "So, the Monday of the convention comes, and in my bag I have a Kerry sign, just that word, ten inches by eight inches. It was a sign issued by the Kerry campaign. I went through the checkpoints and they took that sign away, which absolutely paralyzed my mind. It was an oxymoron that you couldn't have a Kerry sign at his convention."

The next day Lavery attended an antiwar event that the American Friends Service Committee was putting on in Boston. "I picked up five

Say No to War signs, which had three-inch sticks on them," he says. "I took the stick off one and put the sign in my pocket. As I went through the inspection at the convention, they took the four away from me."

But he still had one left. So he says he wrote on the back of it: "DNC would not allow this sign!"

"I then moved around almost the entire convention, standing in front of each delegation," he says. "The DNC sent out two employees, who surrounded me with Kerry/Edwards signs to block me. I said, 'The two of you should be ashamed of yourselves.' I asked one of them, 'Why are you doing this?'

" 'We have to keep signs away from the TV cameras.'

"I said, 'Who instructed you to follow me?'

"His answer was, 'I can't say.' "

Lavery did not buy the argument that everyone in the hall should fall in lockstep behind Kerry.

"Unity doesn't mean giving up your First Amendment rights. And it doesn't mean we all need to act like robots," he says. "I'm disappointed at my party and my candidate, who I'm working for. And I'm a little frightened about the ramifications that go with this. If this happens on the floor of a Democratic Party convention, and no one is riled, and it is permitted by the highest authorities of the party, and none of the media pay attention, then it has certain portents for the future of free speech."

I tried to get a comment from the DNC. One press spokesperson told me on background that they had to check "anything that was being brought in and out for security reasons."

4. Evicted for Wearing "Protect Our Civil Liberties" Shirts—
Candice Julian, Tania Tong, and Janet Voorhies

On October 14, 2004, three teachers in Oregon decided to go to a Bush event wearing shirts that read simply, "Protect Our Civil Liberties."

The rally was at the Jackson County Fairgrounds near Medford, where they teach. They wanted to see their president, and they also wanted to stand up for First Amendment rights, since they had heard on NPR that the Bush campaign was curtailing such rights all along the trail.

So they came up with an ingenious idea. They obtained tickets for the event, and they made and wore T-shirts that said "Protect Our Civil Liberties." Alas, they were not allowed to hear the president. In fact, they were threatened with arrest.

I talked with two of the three teachers, Tania Tong and her sister, Candice Julian, both of whom teach special education to elementary school children in Medford. The third is a student teacher named Janet Voorhies, who works with Tong. "We didn't want to come up with anything that was offensive or antagonistic," says Julian, who says it was her idea to have the shirts say "Protect Our Civil Liberties." "We were concerned about stories we had heard about people trying to go to participate in rallies and being denied access because they had paraphernalia that said something about Kerry," Tong explains. "We wanted to voice our opinion in a way that wasn't degrading to anybody. The shirt was really kind of benign."

They got tickets ahead of time and proceeded to the fairgrounds. They showed their driver's licenses and tickets at the first checkpoint. Campaign officials "were scrutinizing our T-shirts," Julian says, but they let the three in.

At the second checkpoint, which consisted of a metal detector staffed by the Secret Service, Tong says more questions arose, such as: "Do you know this is a Bush rally?" and "Are you going to vote for Bush?"

The campaign officials said the teachers could go in if they could guarantee they would not make a scene, Tong says. "We assured them that we did not come with any intention of being disorderly, so they said fine, and said they respected our differing opinions," she recalls.

At that point, the three teachers assumed they were in and that they could take their seats and listen to the president. Campaign officials did not leave the three alone, however. They followed them to their seats, and when Janet Voorhies got up to go to the bathroom, she was tailed, Tong and Julian say. When Voorhies did not return promptly they became concerned and got up to see what was going on.

"A guy had Janet by the elbow and was leading her away," says Julian. "And he said to us, 'Give us your tickets.' We said, 'Why?' And I put the ticket behind my back, and one of the guys who had been following us ripped it out of my hands."

"They said it was a private event, for invited guests," Tong recalls. "We said we were invited because we were given tickets."

"You don't have tickets anymore," they responded.

"We did until you ripped them out of our hands."

Tong asked if their shirts had caused offense. One of the men, she remembers, called the shirts "obscene."

5. Secret Service Asks About Photographer's Race—Mamta Popat

Mamta Popat is a photographer for the *Arizona Daily Star*. On July 30, 2004, the day before Dick Cheney appeared in Tucson for a campaign rally, the Bush-Cheney campaign "insisted on knowing the race" of Popat, who was assigned to cover the event, the paper reported.

The paper had already provided the usual kind of clearance information. "We had gone through the normal chain, where we submit our name, Social Security number, and date of birth," says Popat, who was not expecting problems. "Around three in the afternoon I got a call for a comment from our political reporter, C.J. Karamargin," she says. "I was just surprised. I didn't know what he was talking about. I couldn't believe it was actually happening, and they were asking that question." Popat talked with the managing editor, Teri Hayt. "She told me to just continue with my job the next day and arrive at the event, and if anything happened, C.J. would be there as well, and we'd see what they say."

That's what she did. "I was able to cover the event with no incident," she says.

Danny Diaz, a spokesman for Bush-Cheney, told the paper that the requested information was "to ensure the safety of all those involved, including the Vice President of the United States." Diaz later told the *Daily Star* he was following the orders of the Secret Service.

The Secret Service denies that racial profiling was involved. Race is a "personal identifier" for obtaining accurate background information, Secret Service spokeswoman Lorie Lewis told Karamargin and the *Daily Star* on August 3. "We aren't using that information for profiling purposes. They are standard checks. The Secret Service does not and will not tolerate racial or cultural bias."

"It was such an outrageous request, I was personally insulted," Hayt said, according to Karamargin's story. Hayt wondered about racial profiling. "Because she has Indian ancestry, were they going to deny her access?"

Popat applauds her paper for standing up for her. "It was great," she says. When she told her colleagues at the South Asian Journalists

Association about the incident "they were outraged," she says. And the Asian American Journalists Association issued a statement expressing shock over the inquiry.

"It's unbelievable," said Mae Cheng, president of the association. "We find it unconscionable that a journalist could be called into question over her race or ethnicity."

Abe Kwok, a vice president of the group, added: "Mamta's race is not relevant, and to ask for it sends a message that certain races represent security risks and are not to be trusted. That is wrong."

The *Daily Star* also revealed on August 3 that the Bush-Cheney campaign had asked about the race of journalists at three other local news outlets.

XV

Goon Violence

1. A Death Foretold—Balbir Singh Sodhi

Balbir Singh Sodhi knew some Sikh would get hurt. He just didn't know it would be him.

Within hours of 9/11 he was telling family members, as well as Guru Roop Kaur Khalsa, a religious leader of the Phoenix Sikh community, that people were not safe.

"We were expecting a backlash," says his brother Rana. "They showed Osama bin Laden with a turban. I'm wearing a turban. And 99 percent of the people wearing turbans in the United States are Sikhs."

The oldest brother in the family, Balbir, fifty-one, called Rana to warn him. "My brother told me, 'If you don't want to go to work, stay home.'" he recalls.

Rana, who also runs a gas station in the Phoenix area, felt the hostility in the air. "People were giving me the finger," he says. "And on the day after 9/11 my brother and I were in his car when someone came up next to us and said, 'Go back to your country, you assholes, you fucking people.'" The next day Balbir and Rana set up a meeting with Guru Roop Kaur Khalsa. "We're going to suffer," they told her, says Rana. "Not our family, but Sikhs will suffer. People see us as out-laws."

Guru Roop Kaur Khalsa confirms this. "Balbir said he was so con-cerned for the safety of others that we needed to do something imme-diately," she says. "He made that appeal. So we sought out a strategy."

They planned to call the media on Sunday, September 16, to ex-plain to them that Sikhs had nothing to do with 9/11, to educate the media about why Sikhs wear turbans, and to notify them that Sikhs were getting a lot of heat.

They didn't get a chance to do that.

On Saturday morning, September 15, Balbir Singh Sodhi went to Costco to buy an American flag to put up at the Mesa gas station that he owned. "He emptied out the money he had in his pocket and put it in the box for the 9/11 victims," says Guru Roop Kaur Khalsa.

That afternoon Balbir Singh Sodhi was shot five times at his gas station. He had been standing outside talking to a landscaper and planting flowers.

His assailant, Frank Roque, said he murdered Sodhi "because he was dark skinned, bearded, and wore a turban." When Roque, who was eventually convicted, was arrested, he said, "I stand for America all the way."

"One of my brother's employees called me and told me there's a shooting at the gas station," Rana says. "I thought it was a minor rob-bery." But when he drove over there, his worst fears were confirmed. "We knew it was going to happen to some of the Sikhs," he says.

"He was such a giver," says Guru Roop Kaur Khalsa. "He'd hand out candy to all the little kids who came into his store, and if a cus-tomer didn't have money for gas, he'd just say, 'Fine, come back later and pay for it.' He had this sense of community. This man cared so much for us."

Less than a year later, unbelievably, Rana lost another brother to violence.

While driving a cab in San Francisco, Sukhpal Singh Sodhi was shot to death.

Police said he was a random victim of stray gang gunfire.

Rana doesn't see it that way. "I believe myself it's 100 percent" a hate crime, he says. He adds that Sukhpal had been beaten the week before in his cab by teenagers making racist comments.

"I lost my two brothers in an eleven-month period," Rana says. "People are ignorant, and that's why I lost my two brothers."

Rana personally encountered this ignorance several times. He says that shortly after Balbir was murdered "someone pulled up in a car and showed me a big knife. And [in 2003] someone painted a swastika in front of my gas station."

To this day Rana says he encounters hostility.

"We still face a lot of trouble," he says. In the spring of 2006 he "was on the freeway and somebody drove up next to me and flashed their flashlight into my face. They were trying to get me into an accident."

Rana says he has received a lot of support from the Phoenix community, and love from his neighbors. And he's grateful for that. Right now he's trying to do his part to educate people, so he visits school classes to talk about who Sikhs are.

"This is a long process," he says. "We need to keep pushing." But he still gets yelled at from total strangers while walking down the street.

"It's very sad when you've been through a lot of those things and it's still happening to you," he says. "I have three kids, eight, ten, and twelve. I want my children to be safer. I don't want them to suffer."

He says his mother wants him to move back to India.

2. Muslim Family Terrorized in Georgia—Mohamed and Sania Kamran

Sania Kamran says it all began at Wal-Mart.

The twenty-seven-year-old mother of four lives in Douglasville, Georgia, about forty-five minutes from Atlanta. Born in Pennsylvania, she describes herself as "white, blond hair, blue eyes." She says she's been a Muslim for about five years, and she's married to a Muslim man who came here from Pakistan.

She shops at her local Wal-Mart several times a week, she says, and it was there that she began noticing the hostility of other customers. Over the course of several months she says she had seen "that snide look" when she was at the store with her young children and her husband, since they are all darker than she is. She says some people would comment on her Muslim attire and ask, "How could you wear something like that?"

Or, she says, they would ask, "Don't you feel bad for making your daughter dress that way?"

She endured these insults until one day in late March 2006.

Here's the Wal-Mart encounter, as she recalls it:

"A customer, an older lady in her mid-sixties, says, 'Ma'am, where are you from?'

"I say, 'Pittsburgh, PA.'

" 'Where is your husband from?'

" 'Pakistan.'

" 'You ought to be ashamed of yourself then.'

" 'Why should I be ashamed of myself?'

" 'Because our forefathers died to give us the rights and freedoms we have, and you're giving it all up by being a Muslim.' "

Kamran says she responded by saying that her father was a Vietnam vet, and that he also served in the Gulf War and Desert Storm. "He served our country for twenty-six years," she recalls saying. "Because of people like my father and others, I have the right to choose who I'm going to pray to and who I'm going to be."

After the conversation ended, Kamran says she didn't pay any mind to it.

A few days later she was back at Wal-Mart, and when she walked out to the parking lot she noticed something. "I went to open up the hatch to our van, and in the dust on the window they'd written 'Killers.' "

She thinks it might have had something to do with the fact that she had "Proud2B a Muslim" written on her license plate frame.

"I was disgusted," she says. "Someone touched my property that had no right to."

She drove home and called her husband, and he told her to "wash it off and just let it go." At that point, she says, she wasn't scared. "OK, they wrote on my car. No big deal," she remembers thinking.

But then, about a week later, in the early morning hours of April 8, it became a big deal.

"I woke up to nurse my eight-month-old," she recalls. "While I was feeding him I heard, like, a pop. I wasn't sure what it was. At first I thought it was my neighbor's car door. Then I saw a flicker, like a flame. I thought some idiot had lit our garbage can as a prank. But then I saw smoke coming out of my van, and I screamed for my husband."

They called 911 and then sat on their front steps and watched the van burn, she says. One fireman drew their attention to something else. "He pointed to our garage, and they had spray painted across it, 'Killers go home.' "

"It felt as if someone had just kicked us in the gut," she says. "What had we done to anybody to deserve that? I sat on our front stoop crying my eyes out."

Kamran says the Douglas County police have been slow to investigate, but the FBI is now on the case. "The preliminary investigation is still ongoing," says Special Agent Stephen Emmett, spokesperson for the FBI's Atlanta office. "Upon its conclusion it will be forwarded to the civil rights division of the Department of Justice in Washington, D.C., for review."

Ibrahim Hooper, communications director of the Council on American-Islamic Relations, says the incident is an example of "growing Islamophobia."

Kamran says she is no longer wearing Muslim garb. "We can't afford to lose another vehicle," she says. "It makes me mad. I'm proud to be who I am and what I am. I shouldn't have to be a Muslim in secret. But my husband said I know who I am inside, and I don't need to advertise it to everybody else."

She wishes, though, that "people would read about our religion and not just believe what they hear on TV," she says. "Everyone thinks now that I'm a Muslim I'm oppressed. It's not like that. My husband treats me wonderfully."

She says her experience has opened her eyes. "It wasn't until I became Muslim that I realized what other minorities feel," she says. "And it's pathetic."

3. Texas Mosque Vandalized with "Sand Niggers" Graffiti— Mohamed El-Moctar

Mohamed El-Moctar is the imam of the Islamic Center of the South Plains in Lubbock, Texas. One day in February 2004, he got a strange phone call. A threatening man asked whether he believed in Jesus and what he thought about Osama bin Laden.

A few weeks later, when El-Moctar arrived for the early morning prayer on Sunday, March 7, 2004, he knew something was amiss. "One of the windows of the mosque was broken, and there was a lot of glass and stone inside the mosque," he says. "My office door was broken, the computers were destroyed, some of my books were torn, and there was some graffiti written inside the office and in the library."

The graffiti included "America rocks, bitch," and "Sand niggers."

"I was shocked," he says. "People are very kind here in Lubbock. I called a few members of the board of the Islamic Center and then called the police department and the FBI."

El-Moctar says the police arrested four young males, and that all four were convicted. They may have been involved in gang activity.

"We got a lot of support from religious leaders in the community," he says. "I'm grateful for that."

Since 9/11, the Council on American-Islamic Relations has recorded dozens of incidents against mosques and Islamic centers in the United States. In August 2003, for example, CAIR issued a statement saying, "Investigators determined that a blaze at the Islamic Center of Savannah in Savannah, GA, was an act of arson. In 2002, a pick-up truck was driven into the front of the Islamic Center of Tallahassee."

The Savannah fire "came after two suspicious incidents" earlier that month, according to the *Savannah Morning News.* "On August 3, five bullet holes were found in the center's garage door. On August 18, the apartment of a student who worships there was burglarized. . . . Left behind was a note with a swastika on it. The note demanded Muslims leave Savannah and said Muslims are being watched '24-7.' "

El-Moctar recalls other incidents at his mosque. A few days after 9/11 he found the following message on the office phone-answering machine: "You Arabs are all guilty. Go back to your ugly countries." He called the police. "They came and they heard the message," he says. "They asked if we had Caller ID. We didn't, but we put it on after that."

Some members of his mosque were also personally victimized in the aftermath of the terrorist attack. "A few days after 9/11 a lady from Egypt whose husband was getting a post-doc at Texas Tech was returning to her apartment at about ten A.M.," he says. "She had a head scarf on, and someone was following her. He entered the apartment behind her, he beat her and tied her to a chair, and he put a gag in her mouth. She was traumatized, and they left the country a few days later."

4. Arsonist Sets Fire to Peace Activists' Porch—
Cindy Hunter and Sam Nickels

Cindy Hunter and her husband, Sam Nickels, opposed Bush's war against Iraq. Even before it started they were putting up an antiwar sign on their property, says Hunter, a professor of social work at James Madison University in Harrisonburg, Virginia.

At first the sign expressed the hope that the war could be avoided.

Then, says Hunter, they changed the sign to list the number of casualties, which they updated periodically, and sometimes to list the number of weapons of mass destruction found, which was always zero. She says the signs provoked a lot of good dialogue. But that's not all.

"People would come by at night every few weeks or so and break our sign up," she says. "And one time last spring we had eggs tossed against our house," which is a few blocks from campus. To spare the sign they decided to bring it up on their porch.

"I attached it to a wood column on the porch, thinking it might be less offensive and more out of the way. I calculated badly on that one," says Nickels, who teaches Spanish in a local middle school.

The final sign they had on their porch read:

8,109 Iraqi civilians.

6,000-plus U.S. wounded.

345 U.S. and British soldiers.

At 4:50 A.M. on October 20, 2003, Hunter and Nickels were asleep. So were their three children, ages seven, eight, and eleven. And so was Adama Sow, a thirty-year-old refugee from Mauritania, who was living upstairs.

"Our smoke alarm went off, and my husband and I got out of bed and saw smoke and got the kids out and our roommate out," Hunter says. "It was immediately clear to me that the sign had burned, because the only fire you could see was on the right front of the house where the sign used to be."

The fire department, from the very beginning, investigated it as a case of arson.

Hunter says the fire cost "about $50,000 in damage. The whole upstairs of our house was charred, and the firemen made a hole in the roof. We lost the kinds of things you carry with you your whole life: papers you wrote in school, or clothes my mom saved for me and I've saved for my grandchildren." But she's just grateful her family and roommate got out safely.

The support from the campus and the Harrisonburg community was "fantastic," she says. On the evening after the fire "seventy or eighty people came to our house and held a candlelight vigil to support us, and to express the outrage that someone would burn our house and put our lives in danger for a political sign." Residents also offered material support to the family. "Students collected gift certificates, many local restaurants donated meals, and storage facilities offered us free space," she says.

On October 22, the *Daily News-Record*, which is a conservative paper, wrote a strong editorial entitled "Arson Assault." It said:

The arson at the home of an anti-war Harrisonburg couple was outrageous and must be condemned not only by those who believe in
the First Amendment, but also by all those who believe in decency
and humanity. The harassment of the Harrisonburg couple was ap-
palling. . . . Violence and vandalism used to intimidate are not only
criminal and cowardly, but profoundly un-American.

On October 28, about 150 people attended a rally on campus to
support the family and free speech. "I Thought This Was America"
one sign said, according to the *Daily News-Record*. And a forum was
held that evening entitled, "Is Silence the Price of Freedom?" One man
wore a shirt with an American flag on it and the words: "This idea
doesn't burn."

Hunter was concerned about the effect the fire has had on Adama
Sow, the refugee who was living upstairs. "This was very difficult for
him, probably more emotionally difficult for him than for us, maybe
because he's already experienced the loss of life due to this kind of ha-
tred," she says. Sow's father, a teacher, was imprisoned and tortured,
and he eventually died from torture-related injuries. Hunter actually
knew Sow's father in Mauritania; she was in the Peace Corps there in
the mid-1980s, and he taught her French.

Sow came to the United States and first lived in New York. But
after 9/11 "we invited him to come down and live with us, because
New York was very expensive, and it was traumatic for him to be
there," Hunter says.

Sow, who is studying computers at James Madison University, is
unsettled by the arson. "It's scary, it's very scary," he says. "It makes
you feel like maybe you have to be very careful."

While Hunter is grateful the community rallied behind her and
her family, she says, "We weren't planning to be the peace poster child
of Harrisonburg."

On November 4, 2003, the *Daily News-Record* reported that this fire was the work of vandalism, not politically inspired violence: "A fire previously believed to have been set by a person opposed to a local family's anti-war beliefs is in fact an act of random violence perpetrated by a teenager, fire officials said."

But Hunter doesn't buy that. "I totally do not believe it was absolutely random," she says. "It was too bad that the press thought it was important to say it had nothing to do with politics."

The culprit was a minor who knew who they were, and knew about their signs.

"We went through a mediation process with the family," Hunter says. "He did say that some adult in his presence had made negative comments about our signs." She says her kids "are a little leery" of having any more signs up on the house.

5. Anti-Bush Sign Torched on Lawn—Joel and Jeanne Kerwin

In the weeks before the 2004 election Joel and Jeanne Kerwin of Whitehouse, New Jersey, wanted to tell their neighbors and anyone else passing by on the busy road outside their house just how they felt.

So they put up a huge canvas sign in mid-October that had yellow ribbons on it indicating support for the troops. The sign, which was about twenty-four feet long and three feet high, said "Save America, Defeat Bush."

The Township of Readington "gave us a summons, because the sign violated a zoning ordinance that says political signs can't be bigger than sixteen square feet," says Jeanne Kerwin, a medical ethicist at Overlook Hospital. "They said they had five complaints about the sign. We didn't argue; the ordinance is the ordinance. But before we took it down, it was stolen."

All that remained was some torn canvas and the poles.

On October 24, the Kerwins put up a second sign that conformed to the size requirements, with the exact same message. "The following morning there was a knock on our door at about six forty-five," Kerwin says. "It was the police. The cop said, 'Your sign is burning.' I looked out, and it was fully engulfed in flames. It was really scary." The fire department came, and the police were called, but they didn't apprehend anyone for the crime.

The Kerwins refused to back down. Her son, Fred True, who had made the two previous signs with some friends, went back to work.

"We said, we're not going to be deterred," she says. "We have a constitutional right, so we put up a third sign: 'Wisdom is better than weapons of war. Rebuild America. Defeat Bush.' "

The line about wisdom is straight out of Ecclesiastes. But that did not impress the vandals.

"On November 1, at about one-fifteen in the morning, I woke up to the sound of a staple gun," Kerwin says. "I looked out the window and saw someone stapling something onto our sign. My husband jumped into his clothes. I was fearful, honestly. I told my husband, 'Be careful. These people are vicious. They're hateful.' I was worried for his well-being, and I was watching from the window. The guy jumped in his car before he got out there. I was relieved, actually. You never know what these people will do."

What they had done was staple eight cardboard posters onto the sign, which covered it all up. And on the cardboard they had written their own political messages. "One of them said 'Ten out of ten terrorists don't want Bush. Vote Bush.' Another one said 'UN sanctions failed. War is the answer.' "

Kerwin's husband ripped the cardboard down, but there was still more trouble before the day was through. That afternoon her husband "saw someone walk up to the sign and start ripping the sign down," she says.

"We live in a very Republican town," says Kerwin, "and I happen to be a registered Republican, though I haven't voted that way the last two times. So I'm not surprised people didn't agree with the sign, but I am dismayed and shocked by the violent and hateful reaction. It's a scary thing, because I think we're losing the integrity of our Constitution. We're going backward. People are going back into savage ways."

6. *An Upside-Down Flag and a Dead Coyote—John Fleming*

John Fleming owns an activist book-and-record store in Alamosa, Colorado. On the day that Bush began bombing Iraq in March 2003, Fleming hung an upside-down flag in the store window of his Roost and Coyote's Den.

"The upside-down flag is a sign of distress in the Boy Scout manual," Fleming says. "And I set out to express my distress over the war." Some outraged residents complained to the police.

"I had a half dozen calls in thirty minutes," Alamosa police chief Ron Lindsey says. Lindsey came over to the store and told Fleming that he couldn't legally have an upside-down flag on display.

"If I take the flag down and buckle under, don't you see what the implications will be?" Fleming recalls asking. "Don't you see what that does to the First Amendment, or has Bush destroyed that already?"

"You know, it's inflaming the community," the police chief said.

Shortly thereafter the ACLU of Colorado threatened to sue, and city attorneys quickly told the police chief he had no legal leg to stand on. Chief Lindsey says he based his action on a flag-desecration statute. "I thought it pertained," he says. "Obviously that was the wrong thing to do."

Fleming's nickname, by the way, is Coyote. During the controversy Sylvia Lobato of the *Alamosa Valley Courier* wrote a story about it, mentioning Fleming's nickname. The next day he found an unwelcome sight waiting for him at the store. "Someone went out and shot a coyote and threw the bleeding carcass up against the front door of the Roost," Fleming told me at the time. "I can't get the blood off the concrete. They took the ears off so they could claim the five-dollar bounty. I took it as a death threat."

Three years later business was still down. "Ever since this incident, I took a big hit economically," says Fleming, who has renamed the store the Coyote's Den and Used Books. "My business just dropped."

XVI

Conclusion

All is not lost. The battle for our civil liberties is ongoing. We have our defeats and our victories. Several of the people I profiled in this book eventually prevailed. And they did so because they fought back. These individuals have not been acting alone, or in a vacuum. Valiant civil liberties groups have been supporting them, such as the ACLU, the Center for Constitutional Rights, the Council on American-Islamic Relations, and the American-Arab Anti-Discrimination Committee. If you like the work they do, support them. They all need the help.

Many grassroots groups have risen to the challenges of our times. One that sticks out is the Bill of Rights Defense Committee out of Northampton, Massachusetts. Founded by Nancy Talanian in November 2001, it pioneered an impressive practice of civic engagement. It prompted city councils and county boards to debate—and ultimately to pass—resolutions affirming the Bill of Rights. Those resolutions put the feds on notice that these local governments will not cooperate in any law enforcement operation under the Patriot Act that violates the rights of their constituents. By July 4, 2006, 399 communities and 8 states had passed such resolutions. (You can find out how to draft such a resolution for your own community at www.bordc.org.)

Nor are we alone in the halls of Congress. A few courageous

elected officials, such as Senators Russ Feingold and Robert Byrd and Representatives John Conyers, Barbara Lee, Dennis Kucinich, and Tammy Baldwin, have been outspoken on these issues. And it's not just a left-right thing. Such Republicans as Representative Ron Paul and Senator Larry Craig have not been taking the assault on civil liberties lying down, even when their own leadership is stampeding the herd.

Surprisingly, the judiciary has occasionally stood up to this renegade administration. That's not always been the case in time of war, as David Cole has noted in *Enemy Aliens*. Many local judges have recognized some of the infringements that I've chronicled here, and they have ruled against the police and in favor of our freedoms. Several appellate court judges have written scalding opinions about the abuses of power the Bush administration has committed. And the U.S. Supreme Court, in two landmark cases, has pulled on the reins. In *Hamdi v. Rumsfeld*, the Court ruled in June 2004 that "enemy combatants" had due process rights. As Justice Sandra Day O'Connor put it in *Hamdi*, "even the war power [of the president] does not remove constitutional limitations safeguarding essential liberties." Two years later, in *Hamdan v. Rumsfeld*, the Court threw out the military tribunals the administration had established at Guantánamo Bay. Justice John Paul Stevens, writing for the Court, said, "The executive is bound to comply with the rule of law"—and with the Geneva Conventions.

A quaint notion, perhaps, but refreshing nonetheless.

What's more, there has been something of a cultural thaw. Bill Maher is back on cable. The Dixie Chicks, who once faced mass hostility, including bonfires of their CDs, have remained defiant and once again have achieved great popularity on the charts. Other musicians, across genres, have spoken out against the Bush administration at no cost. Keith Olbermann on MSNBC rails against the president and gets a larger audience for it. Jon Stewart regularly skewers Bush, as does

David Letterman. And Stephen Colbert even spoofed the president of the United States to his face at the White House Correspondents' Dinner.

In communities across the country there appears to be some more space for dissent. When Lisa Jensen and Bill Trimarco of Loma Linda, Colorado, put up a Christmas wreath in the shape of a peace symbol on their house in November 2006, they were threatened by the Loma Linda Homeowners Association with a $25-a-day fine. But the local outcry was so fierce that the board members of the homeowners association had to back down, apologize, and resign. Other residents nearby began putting up their own peace wreaths in solidarity.

There is one exception to this trend, a telling one: for Arabs and Muslims in the United States, not much has changed. At the same time that the Loma Linda residents rose up to defend their free speech rights, six imams were handcuffed and booted off a US Airways flight in Minneapolis after complaints that they were praying onboard.

"It's as bad as after 9/11," said Rana Abbas-Chami of the Michigan American-Arab Anti-Discrimination Committee, in a front-page story in *USA Today* on December 13, 2006. "A lot of people are scared." The Council on American-Islamic Relations reports that anti-Muslim incidents increased by 30 percent from 2004 to 2005.

Despite all the assaults on our liberties, I remain hopeful.

As the historian Howard Zinn teaches us in his wonderful memoir, *You Can't Be Neutral on a Moving Train,* "To be hopeful in bad times is not just foolishly romantic. It is based on the fact that human history is a history not only of cruelty, but also of compassion, sacrifice, courage, kindness. . . . If we remember those times and places—and there are so many—where people have behaved magnificently, this gives us the energy to act, and at least the possibility of sending this spinning top of a world in a different direction."

A little story to end with: A couple of years ago I was asked to speak at the community center of a senior citizens facility in Madison, Wisconsin, on the very topic of this book: the assaults on our civil liberties. It was a good crowd, very attentive. One woman, up in the front row on the left, asked several probing questions. She expressed outrage at Bush's policies, and at the fear they were causing. As things were winding down I said I'd take two more questions. She was the second one to raise her hand, so I called on her last. And she said, "Can I get *The Progressive* in a plain brown wrapper?"

If you feel you need to read this book in a plain brown wrapper, we're worse off than I thought.

Flaunt your freedoms.